PREHISTORIC HERITAGE

PREHISTORIC
HERITAGE

by Felix R. Paturi
translated by
Tania and Bernard Alexander

Charles Scribner's Sons · New York

Originally published as
Zeugen der Vorzeit
Copyright © 1976 by Econ Verlag GmbH, Dusseldorf and Vienna

Translation copyright © 1979 by Macdonald and Jane's, London

First American edition
Published by Charles Scribner's Sons 1979

1 3 5 7 9 11 13 15 17 19 I/C 20 18 16 14 12 10 8 6 4 2

Printed in Great Britain

Library of Congress Catalog Card Number 79-84389

ISBN 0-684-16279-2

CONTENTS

INTRODUCTION

This is not a text-book on prehistoric archaeology, nor is it a comprehensive survey of everything that has happened in Europe in 'prehistoric times'. Anyone who by chance has come across 'silent witnesses of the past' on a journey to the north, south or west of the European Continent, or seen pictures in tourist brochures or photographs taken by friends on holiday, will learn from this book what it is that he has seen. Those who have admired the cave paintings in the south of France and would like to find out how many thousands of years ago they were executed; or how excavators can be certain of the exact data which they have collected; or what the mysterious stone blocks in Sardinia and Mallorca signify, will find the answers in this book. Further, anyone who intends to spend his vacation in Scotland, Spain, Sicily or Denmark searching for traces of prehistoric times will find this book packed with valuable information.

This book is meant for those who are fascinated by the recently developed research techniques and their amazing 'results'; and for those who are drawn to the mysterious.

Finally, those who from childhood have dreamed of the chance, if only once in a lifetime, of seeing the towering stones on Easter Island or the mysterious rock carvings in the southern Sahara, but cannot afford the luxury of travel to far off places, will find that they can discover traces of the past without having to journey so far afield. Every mountain, valley, moor, steppe and grotto throughout Europe carries thousands of fascinating traces and testimonials of ancient times.

PREHISTORIC
TIMES

Mysterious Traces of Prehistory

Mallorca in September. A late summer heat lies over the Garriga, which is a parched savannah, covered with knee-high grass, to the south and east of the island. On it can be seen the withered long stems of a flat, spindly thistle, called asphodel, which crackles underfoot; isolated semi-circular clumps of bushy dwarf palm-trees, and, clinging to every stem, to every blade of grass, countless little snail shells bleached by the sun. The earth is cracked. A lizard appears between the myriad fragments of limestone which are the size of a fist, or even of a human head. In the heat of the day the shrill, monotonous tones of the chirping crickets seem to blend with the shimmering atmosphere. The traveller is filled with a sense of timelessness, and is suddenly aware of being in the presence of a silent witness from an era long past: a talayot, unfamiliar and forbidding, rises out of the undergrowth. Its mute magnitude and immobility fit well into the landscape. It belongs here.

Nothing but its very existence connects it with the present. They must have been a race of giants who piled the huge lumps of rock on top of each other to construct these cyclopean walls. When? How? And why?

At one time there must have been easily a thousand of these strange tors in Mallorca. Today some thirty of them are still in a more or less good state of preservation. Most of them cannot be found on any road map, however detailed, nor is there any mention of them in any travel guide to the island. They are the enigmatic vestiges of a grey, prehistoric time.

1 The talayot of San Canova on Mallorca, 8 kms west of Artá on the little road to Colonia de San Pedro, is one of the few in the form of a square. The more typical ones on this island are nearly always circular.

2   *This Corsican menhir stands like a sentinel from the distant past in a shaded grove by the Romanesque church of Santa Maria*

Corsica in March. The narrow and poorly paved road winds through the rugged and mountainous landscape. Every now and then the car passes through short avenues of blossoming eucalyptus trees, which give off a bitter scent like the smell of cough pastilles. Tall, bright yellow acacia trees, resembling mimosa bushes, flash by in sharp contrast to the clear blue of the spring sky. The tops of the mountains are still white with the winter snows.

Immediately after a turning to the right, south of the mountain village of San Lorenzo, there stands the Romanesque church of Santa Maria. A narrow and partly hidden path cuts through the maquis, an impenetrable, rambling thicket made of tree-high shrubs, thorny broom, evergreen oak and more than a dozen other thorny or spiky plants which are intertwined with each other and bound together with yards of climbing bramble. The path climbs on upwards. Four or five noble chestnut trees dominate a small clearing. From here the remains of an earlier road can be seen: then more maquis. It is not until you stand immediately in front of it that you can see the Romanesque church. Next to it there should be a menhir statue, a prehistoric stone figure more than two metres tall, but it is hard to make it out amid the tangled vegetation. Nor can the menhir be seen until you stand immediately in front of it. In the half light created by the tall trees it has an ominous appearance. Deep shadows envelop the huge rough-hewn stone column, emphasizing the stylized face at the top. Above the massive chin there is an open hollow mouth, devoid of lips or teeth. There is only the mere suggestion of a nose, above which there are two expressionless empty holes to denote the eyes.

This is not the only menhir in Corsica. Archaeologists have found dozens of these figures. The maquis certainly hides a great many more. How old could they be? Who carved them out of the stone and why? Why are statues very much like them found in North America? What do these figures represent, these mysterious remains of misty prehistoric days?

*   *   *

About halfway between the lakes of Como and Garda lies Lake Iseo, which just a little more than ten years ago was still a secret refuge to be shared only with enthusiasts who loved camping or sailing on mountain lakes. The treacherous winds sweeping off the nearby sheer rock walls can cause many a close call to the amateur sailor. But today just as many tourists flock to these once secluded shores as to the other lakes of northern Italy.

Only a few kilometres further north the countryside is really peaceful, even if the road from the little town of Edolo is very busy, mostly with through traffic. The villages between Edolo and the lake lying 56 kilometres to the south have not lost any of their original character. Tightly packed against each other, the multi-storied houses with their dirty façades crowd the narrow little streets. Stone fountains, badly in need of repair, decorate the little squares of the village, while in front of the numerous inns and cafés, men of every age loafing or leaning against a wall are a common sight.

One of these villages is Capo di Ponte, 20 kilometres south of Edolo. Prehistorians all over the world know the name because, in the hills around Capo di Ponte, there are small, stylized rock carvings of a runic character which cast a strange and peaceful spell. They are called 'Pitoti' by the natives. Smoothed and rounded in the Ice Age, they are to be found in their thousands in the 'glacier gardens' among the rocks of this valley. They appear in the valley, and continue up the mountains to a height of about 900 metres. They depict people: warriors with helmets and shields, riders with huge spears led by shield-bearers, even ritual dancers and powerful gods. They also portray horses and carts, dogs and hunted stags, lake dwellings, musical instruments of prehistoric times, hundreds of symbolic suns and ritualistic spades, spoked wheels and daggers.

Similar rock carvings can be found in other parts of the Valcamonica, the valley in which Capo di Ponte lies. Today the existence of some 130,000 of these carvings is known. Are they in fact only the scrawls of the 'Camuni', the early

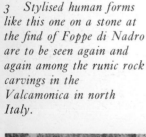

3   Stylised human forms like this one on a stone at the find of Foppe di Nadro are to be seen again and again among the runic rock carvings in the Valcamonica in north Italy.

inhabitants of this mountain valley, or are they carvings of a profound cultural significance? Why is it that 40,000 very similar carvings can be found 300 kilometres away, in the French Alpes Maritimes, on Mont Bégo, nearly 3,000 metres high, on the very edge of the ice cap?

This is not the only mystery. 1,400 kilometres away in southern Sweden there are rocks near what today is called Tanum, where 280 carvings can be seen, some of which almost exactly resemble the figures in the Valcamonica. The same applies to what is the present county of Yorkshire, 1,200 kilometres away. What is the real meaning of these mysterious traces of prehistoric times?

*   *   *

The traveller who leaves the little industrial town, Dol-de-Bretagne, in northern France and continues southwards on Route Nationale 795, will notice not far beyond the last houses a colossal elongated stone in the middle of an old orchard. The unusual feature in this case is that the stone is standing upright. Some 9.5 metres high, it reaches into the air to the height of a three-storey house (see ill. 5). It weighs over

4 The carved rocks in the Valcamonica are usually large blocks which were worn smooth by the force of the glaciers during the Ice Age. For a long time Professor Anati has been trying to pierce the secrets of these rocks.

5 The gigantic menhir of Champ Dolent stands on the southern edge of the little town of Dol-de-Bretagne in Brittany. Its impressive size of 9.5 metres is illustrated by the contrasting height of the author beside it.

150 tons. It was put up without the help of cranes, with only the most primitive resources – three or four thousand years ago.

Yet this is not the largest known menhir, the name given to these prehistoric stone columns. Not far from Locmariaquer, a Breton fishing village, lies a fallen menhir 20 metres long. It weighs not less than 350 tons. When, in 1836 several thousand years later the obelisk from Luxor, weighing 200 tons, was erected in the Place de la Concorde, Parisians celebrated the event as an exceptional technical feat.

But in Brittany there are many smaller menhirs grouped in large numbers. In fact, the famous rows of stones in Carnac alone contain more than 3,000 of them.

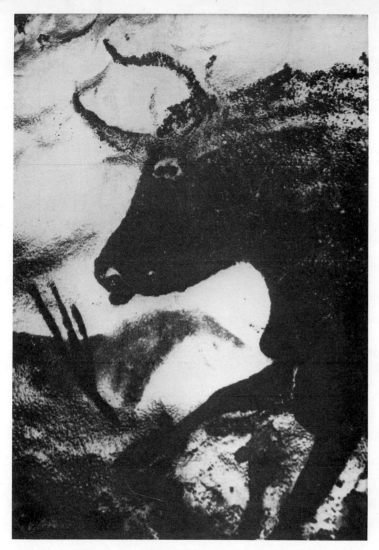

*6   15,000 years ago men
of the Ice Age painted the
picture of this black cow on
the walls of the innermost
part of the caves of
Lascaux; it is an expressive
picture full of life and
strength.*

One could go on almost endlessly with descriptions of
mysterious remains of prehistoric times located over the
whole of Europe. There are still 24,000 stone 'dolmen'
preserved in Denmark today, as well as huge barrows, stone
circles, and other prehistoric monuments. The traveller to
Sardinia can find some 7,000 cyclopean towers peculiar to the
island – the nuraghi. It is certain that originally there were a
great many more than this. In the area of Dronten in eastern
Holland, vast sepulchral mounds, gigantic rock fragments
piled up by prehistoric man, can be found in many places.
Similar constructions are scattered over the whole of northern
Germany. In the British Isles, as far north as the Shetlands,
there are thousands of such stone emplacements: they can also

be found in Spain and Portugal. In the south and east of the Iberian peninsula there are a great many rocks in ravines and cliff walls which are covered with stylized carvings. These are of a different character from those in the Valcamonica in Italy. A comparison clearly shows that they date from different periods. The cave paintings at Lascaux in south-west France and Altamira in northern Spain (see ill. 6) are well known, and there are some ten dozen more paintings in other caves. Southern Italy also has similar caves with paintings, two of which are in Sicily.

There are indeed many remains and examples. So far by no means all have been discovered. No other continent has as many and as varied unsolved riddles from prehistoric times as Europe. The first fascinating steps to solve these mysteries have only just begun to be taken, and the light is only beginning to be shed.

What is 'Prehistory'?
When a detective arrives at the scene of a crime he is confronted at first with what would seem to be an almost arbitrary collection of articles. There seems to be no link between any of them. Nor is it clear in what sequence they had been used, especially when there are no witnesses to the events under investigation.

For a layman the position is a hopeless one. But out of the seemingly unconnected pieces of evidence and clues the experienced detective attempts a reconstruction, giving the time of the crime, its duration, its motivation and execution. A systematic approach, professional experience, and scientific methods of analysis will help him. After many hours and days of tireless work he comes forward with the answer: this is what must have happened; or, this is what might have happened; but this is definitely not what actually happened. And occasionally he may even state that it is not possible to say anything for certain.

The researcher into prehistory is confronted with problems very similar to those faced by the detective. He finds clue after clue. Some are right under his nose, some he must look for or excavate. All are unrelated to each other. At best there may be a geographical connection; sometimes during excavations there are indications of a time sequence. Hardly ever is there any written proof, and if there is, it is only in the shape of strange stones covered with runic carvings, or, in the very late period of prehistory, of second-hand reports by Greek or Roman historians.

The more clues that are available, the more confused the

picture becomes, and the more difficult it is to find in them some kind of logical pattern. This is especially true when it is possible to reconstruct not merely one but a dozen events which need not necessarily have taken place at the same time. Successive generations will often have used the same objects. Then the clues become confused, overlap, and lead to false conclusions.

The researcher into prehistory is interested in ancient cultures which followed upon each other in a small area, infiltrated each other, fought or merged with each other. They all left behind remains which are bound together and need to be systematically unravelled with love and care. Later ethnological groups confused these remains by covering them with their own marks and sometimes by destroying the originals completely.

Scientific interest in prehistory began relatively late, at a time when there is no doubt that a great deal of good, useful material had been lost for ever. At the turn of the 18th century, under the influence of the Romantic movement, scholars of many different subjects began to look into and interpret universal history, starting from an existing object. When they began to search into the meaning of the vast number of pieces of evidence of prehistoric times, they found that peasants, settlers and above all the Christian Church had by that time done their work of muddling up the clues for at least a century and a half. And so, thousands of stone circles, dolmen, and towers were used to provide the materials for the building of walls in fields, sheds, houses, and for strengthening roads. Towns and villages grew without caring for the preservation of any kind of evidence of prehistoric cultures. They were simply covered up. In the Middle Ages the clergy did not rest until they had either completely eradicated the old heathen sanctuaries, or, if popular traditional beliefs forcibly resisted their destruction, had them converted into Holy Christian places. Today chapels and churches are often found on sites which were once ancient places of worship, graves or religious assembly centres. Even in the 17th century religious sculptors converted the archaic hallowed stones into Christian altars by carving on them scenes from the Passion of Christ. It is only in the waste land, steppes, mountains, moors and caves that the ancient remains have been preserved in the state in which they survived throughout the centuries.

At the end of the 18th and the beginning of the 19th century, the first serious investigators into prehistory were faced with an unenviable task. They tried to bring order out of the confusion, but had to do so without the assistance of tested

7   All over Europe during the Middle Ages the Christian Church conducted a tireless campaign against the widely practiced worship of pagan shrines. The princes of the Church removed or destroyed many of the old sacred stones, others were re-dedicated with emblems of the Cross, Christian symbols and sculptures. In this way they guided stubborn reverence for prehistoric heathen shrines into new religious channels. This is the menhir of St. Duzec near Ploemeur–Bodou in Brittany, rededicated into a christian monument.

techniques and the wealth of experience which modern archaeologists have at their disposal. Their main activity was to collect, observe and compare, and after several decades of work a rough sequence of events was established.

In 1836, a year of a great many discoveries, the Danish researcher into early history, Christian Jürgensen Thomsen, published a work of some 36 pages entitled *Clues to the science of Nordic antiquity*, a work which was to be the subject of lively discussion for half a century. In the same year Faraday discovered the chemical power of electricity; Runge discovered aniline; Gauss explained the earth's magnetic fields; Flourens proved that the control of human breathing was located in the brain; Braille had just invented his embossed printing for the blind. During his many excavations Thomsen had found prehistoric stone tools, bronze swords and iron objects. For this reason he put forward the suggestion that prehistory could be divided into the Stone, Bronze and Iron Ages. The experts vehemently contradicted Thomsen's interpretation. Only when more material proving his point was assembled, and when in some places scientists discovered finds in different layers – stone tools on the bottom layer, bronze implements on the next, and only in the topmost layers objects made of iron – only then was the Three Age System generally accepted as definitive. This happened about 1890, when Thomsen had already been dead for 25 years.

The extent to which the Middle Ages had obscured any understanding of early history with their deep-rooted rejection of everything pagan is shown by the fact that the 19th century discovery of the three periods – the Stone, Bronze, Iron Ages – produced neither anything new or sensational. There is no doubt that the scholars of Roman history in the period before Christ knew of this division.

Three-quarters of a century before Christ the Roman poet Lucretius wrote in his work on the nature of things: 'The oldest of all weapons were hands, nails and toes, then came stones, broken-off branches, flame throwers and fire as soon as they were discovered. Only later came the use of iron and bronze. But the use of bronze is older than that of iron, because bronze is easier to shape and easier to obtain. It was only very gradually that the iron sword came into general use as the chief weapon.'

The first of the three periods, the Stone Age, presented archaeologists with very different fragments of evidence. In Denmark Thomsen had found carefully polished stone axes which, judging by the geological layers from which he dug them, must have been several thousand years old. In France the prehistorians came across roughly hewn stone tools which quite certainly were incomparably older. The division into the Old and New Stone Ages was introduced in 1865 by Sir John Lubbock, later Lord Avebury, in his book *Prehistoric Times*. Nevertheless, like all contemporary men of learning, he preferred more learned Greek terms and spoke of Palaeolithicum ('palaios'=old and 'lithos'=stone) and Neolithicum ('neos'=new). 27 years later, another Englishman, Alan Brown, added yet another sub-division, Mesolithicum, the Middle Stone Age. This period was placed between the other two, since there were stone tools and implements among the findings which did not necessarily fit into either of the other eras. By the beginning of this century the time sequence was established: Old Stone Age, Middle Stone Age, New Stone Age, Bronze Age, Iron Age. As is the case in many areas of science, the scholars of this period had discovered what seemed to them an irrefutable structure for the different periods. Based on this they could now go on to specialized studies. While this fostered a meticulous and laborious technique of detailed study, it did not encourage further research into broadly unifying concepts. When, in the 1940s, the Spanish philosopher and writer Ortega y Gasset condemned specialization as a form of barbarism, he said that specialists considered their onesidedness as a great asset and condemned the study of general scientific principles as a form of dilettantism. These remarks applied equally well to the archaeologists of his time. It was only in the middle of this century that there was a greater readiness to establish scientific co-operation between scholars in different branches of science. This made it possible to establish more accurately dates relating to events in prehistoric times, and proved that the rigid sub-division of the earlier prehistoric period which had been firmly accepted in all text-books was not in fact particularly well founded. It is true that tools made of stone are older than those made of bronze and that our ancestors discovered iron after bronze. But it did not follow that a firm division of time into periods could be linked with the different materials. Metal was already in everyday use in the Near East around 3500 B.C. At that time it also found its way into ancient European cultures, at first only as an incidental souvenir. Only later was it used and worked on in its own right. On the island of Crete their actual Bronze Age began around 2500 B.C., and in central Europe only three-quarters of a century later. By the year 1000 B.C. iron had come into general use, but in that same period bronze continued to be used for a long time.

It is therefore not possible to establish firm and universal datelines between the Stone and Bronze Ages and the Bronze and Iron Ages. There was, for example, no 'New' Stone Age whatsoever in the Iberian peninsula. From the beginning, polished tools made of stone and objects made of bronze were used simultaneously. A clear division into three periods is most easily established in the cultures of the northern countries of Europe. In what we call the Latin countries, which are situated closer to Asia Minor, the birthplace of the Bronze Age, this division is much more complex. No wonder, then, that in the literature of the Latin countries there is prevalent an interpretation of prehistory which introduces between the 'New' Stone Age and the Bronze Age a period called Chalcolithicum. In this age copper was already being used as well as stone implements, and this simultaneous use differed in time from area to area. A division according to the use of implements and tools of the prehistoric period is only one of many. Just as paintings are on the one hand classified according to the way in which the artist uses his material, into oil paintings, water-colours, tempera paintings, acrylic-paint pictures, they are also, according to their artistic style, divided into Renaissance, Baroque or Impressionist paintings. They are further divided, according to the tools used, into pencil drawings, brush or palette techniques and finally, depending on the artists, into the works of Italian, Spanish, Russian or Dutch masters.

In the same way there are many different divisions which can be applied to the remains which our forefathers have left behind. Every branch of research pursues a different line of interest, and scientists therefore have been able to exhaust most hypotheses. It is quite legitimate for an ethnologist to be passionately interested in the migration of the ancient Mediterranean peoples; he would, however, not have much time for the way in which these people may have used their tools. In the same way prehistoric wars are not the chief concern of art historians.

All this is quite a serious problem for the layman. For how can he get an overall view of things when no-one can tell him accurately when the Bronze Age actually took place; when he suddenly learns that there is not only an Old, Middle and New Stone Age (Palaeolithic, Mesolithic and Neolithic period), but also a Megalithic culture, the 'great' stone culture (the prefix 'mega' denotes 'great' or 'huge'), which overlaps partly into the New Stone Age and partly into the Bronze Age? The layman may find himself facing a vast stone formation in the south of England and be told 'This is a Megalithic monument', or 'This is an example of the late Neolithic period and was completed in the early Bronze Age', or 'This is a holy shrine of the Druids, a Celtic priesthood'. And all three remarks could refer to the same construction. But do not be put off by names. They have more sound than sense and are not always indispensable for a proper understanding of the traces of the past. They merely simplify discussion for the experts. Anyone who wishes to go further into the subject will not be satisfied with this book. He will want to research other sources which are listed on page 267.

For a first excursion along the trails into ancient Europe, it is enough to know that in professional circles four classifications have generally been accepted. They are:

1   according to the materials used and the ways in which they
    are worked,
2   according to cultural developments,
3   according to the shapes of tools,
4   according to ethnic groups.

So far we have looked at the structure of prehistory through
the eyes of the scholar. But what does the concept 'prehistory'
mean to the scientist? Can there be a time before time? The
definition is simple yet unclear. Prehistory is the period in the
history of man of which there are no written records. This is
easily said. But what are written records? Written characters
were after all not invented from one day to the next. When the
French scholars coined the expression *préhistorique* in 1833
they thought of writing only in the form of letters of the
alphabet. But one of the most widespread scripts in the world
is Chinese, a pictograph script which, in fact, is writing in
images. But are the Chinese of the 20th century therefore a
prehistoric people? Surely not. Communication by symbols
certainly existed in the New Stone Age and in the Bronze Age,
and possibly earlier in the Middle Stone Age. In the ancient
runic signs we even come across early written forms. Ever
since we began to understand the signs on stones the word
'prehistory', invented in 1851 by Daniel Wilson, has little
meaning. Modern research into symbols has reduced it to an
absurdity. But we know what is meant even without being
able to give the word an exact definition. The word prehistory
has become a firm idea in our language.

**Nuclear Physicists, Doctors and Astronomers working
as Detectives on Prehistoric Times**
In southern Canada where the St. John river constitutes the
boundary between Canada and the United States lies the little
town of Edmundston. There lived Wilfrid Bouchard, builder
of wells and fountains, with his wife, his 15-year-old son Jean
Guy and his 16-year-old daughter Gaetane. The calendar on
the kitchen wall showed the date 13th May 1958. The time
was 4.30 p.m. The 16-year-old Gaetane came home from
school to ask her mother for the 10 dollars pocket money she
had been promised. With the money this lively brunette
teenager went out to do a little shopping. In spite of her
cheerfully unkempt appearance she already had a distinctly
feminine air. 'I shall be back for supper by six at the latest,'
she called to her mother on her way out. At six o'clock

Gaetane still had not returned. At 11.30 p.m. her parents were still waiting for her. Her father decided to notify the police. Constable Latour immediately sent out several police cars into the streets of the little town of only 12,000 inhabitants. But it was not his men who finally found the girl, but her brother who, together with his father and a neighbour, had gone out on an independent search party. In a deserted gravel pit which was only occasionally visited in the evenings by young lovers, Jean Guy stumbled upon a shoe belonging to his missing sister. It was a blue leather slipper. Only a few yards away the murdered Gaetane lay on the gravel. In the light of his torch they could see several stab wounds on her chest and back. Her bare legs were covered in scratches. The murderer must have dragged his victim along the gravel. Further evidence of this was a large dark patch about eight yards away where blood had penetrated the stones.

Barely 24 hours later in the small neighbouring town of Madawasca, across the border, a 20-year-old newspaper reporter and acting director of civil defence, John Vollman, was arrested by the C.I.D. on suspicion of murder. A year earlier 'Johnny' had played the saxophone in the Lido dance-hall at Edmundston where he had met Gaetane. Since then he had only been back to the Canadian town very occasionally. However, on the day of the murder, eyewitnesses had seen him there driving his bright green Pontiac with a young girl.

Several clues pointed to John Vollman being the culprit, but there was not sufficient evidence to secure a conviction. A second autopsy on the body showed something which was to become the central *corpus delicti* in the case, although at first it seemed an unimportant discovery: in the fingers of her right hand the dead girl held a single black hair, three inches long. Did it come from the head of the suspect?

The chemical and physical methods of analysing hair which had only been developed some fifty years ago and were used by criminologists were insufficient to provide conclusive evidence on the basis of one hair. They could at best have proved that this hair had not come from the head of the suspect, but if it was very much like his hair it could also have come from anyone else with similar hair. No laboratory test at the time could have proved more even if there had been more hair available for a careful analysis. There was, however, a new and different method of investigation which so far had never been applied to a criminal case. Six years earlier the Canadian Chalk River nuclear research centre, under the direction of Dr. W.M. Campbell, had begun a new pro-gramme of investigation. The work was referred to as the

N.A.A. (neutron activation analysis). The name gives an indication of the process involved.

Nature has two different forms of chemical elements, the normal element and the radio-active one such as Radium or Uranium 235. The radio-active substances send out a special kind of continuous radiation. When a normal element which does not emit radiation is brought into a nuclear reactor, it is subjected to a neutron bombardment and thereby acquires energy and in time changes into a radio-active element. The neutrons have 'activated' it. The radiation emitted by such an element which has artificially been made radio-active can be measured and recorded. At the same time the nuclear physicist is able to discover accurately which element he is concerned with and to assess from the intensity of the radiation how much of this element is present in a sample.

For the first time it was now possible to prove the existence of the tiniest quantity of a chemical element, the so-called 'trace-element'. Neutron activation analysis has been a powerful addition to analytical techniques. By this method it is now possible to find traces in some substances even as minute as a billionth of a gramme of gold.

With this new technique the scientists of Chalk River, together with the Canadian police, examined the single hair taken from the hand of the murdered girl and compared it with some of John Vollman's hair. The two tests showed that almost equal amounts of sulphur and phosphorus were contained in both. Dozens of comparative analyses made with hair taken from other young men, on the other hand, produced negative results. When, on 18th November, Vollman was confronted in court with the results of the analyses, his counsel gave up, and finally he did himself. Until then he had vehemently denied his guilt. In the light of the damning evidence of the N.A.A., he signed a confession. The jury pronounced a verdict of guilty and recommended death by hanging. In February 1959, Vollman's sentence was commuted to life imprisonment.

Reactions to the case of Gaetane Bouchard reverberated wildly in international publications on criminology. But in the late 1950s reports on N.A.A. had an equally sensational effect in quite another profession: archaeology. Two years before the sensational Canadian murder case, their first great success with neutron activation analysis had been reported by Edward Sayre and Richard Dodson of the Brookhaven National Laboratory. The two scientists had been able to establish the precise origin of their archaeological finds by exactly determining trace elements in fragments of the fired clay. If the results of the analysis of the materials correspond to the composition of fragments of pottery from a different site, it is possible to say with certainty that goods must have been transported between the two places. Two different pieces of pottery made out of the same clay can only have been fired in one place and not separately in the various places where they were excavated.

It is not by chance that archaeologists employ the same scientific methods as criminologists. Their task of deciphering archaeological discoveries is similar to that of a detective.

It is as the 'legal expert' in archaeology that the nuclear physicist speaks when it comes to making a judgement on historical or prehistorical finds. N.A.A. is one of several different scientific methods used. Another equally sensitive method of establishing definite clues is the so-called spark-source mass spectrometry. In a much diluted atmosphere the scientist bombards a specimen of his material with a hot electric spark. A part of the substance vaporizes and immediately acquires an electric charge. The movement of the charged particles can be accelerated by means of a magnet to form a curve. The lighter the particles the wider the curve. Fast-moving heavy particles are not so easily forced into a curve due to their inertia. The charged particles are separated during their curved flights into different groups according to their weight. The heavier ones leave the curved trajectory first and the lighter ones last. This process accurately reveals to the scientist the masses of the individual particles. The masses infallibly prove from which chemical element each particle originates. Like N.A.A., the neutron activation process of analysis, this form of analysis is equally useful in tracing the composition of a fragment from an archaeological discovery. Thomas J. Cairns, a scholar at the Museum of Art in Los Angeles, has been using this method for years in his examinations of ancient bronze discoveries. Both these examples explain why scholars of prehistory are often able to give precise information about the old trade routes or even about the methods used in making prehistoric utensils.

Yet another process was the complicated Mössbauer-spectrometry. By this method the British scientists D.R. Cousins and K.G. Dharmawardena only recently established the temperature used in kilns for making old ceramics. Both scholars are convinced that one day it will be possible to re-create the exact process used in firing the clay.

Modern methods of research into prehistory use some of the processes of nuclear physics to establish accurately the age of many finds. The best-known is the C-14 process, the fruit of extensive atomic research undertaken during and immediately after the Second World War.

Every chemist knows that C stands for carbon. C-14 is a very special form of carbon. Its atomic nucleus consists of 14 elementary particles whereas ordinary carbon is made up of only 12. The carbon 14 atom is unstable and disintegrates in the course of time. During this process it emits radio-active rays and turns into the ordinary carbon 12. Both types of carbon can fuse with other chemical elements; for example in combination with oxygen it becomes carbon dioxide gas, which is, of course, a constituent element of the atmosphere. The C-14 content of the atmosphere has helped nuclear physicists to discover two interesting facts which would seem at first glance to be contradictory.

1   The concentration of carbon 14 in the air always remains the same (insofar as this is not disturbed by man-made atomic experiments).

2   Out of every ton of C-14 90 grammes disintegrate every year.

Both observations can only be reconciled with each other if as many new C-14 atoms are constantly being formed somewhere in the world as are disintegrating. This does in fact happen. C-14 is found in the upper strata of the atmosphere because of an exchange which goes on between the air and the radio-active rain of neutrons coming from the universe. In the carbon dioxide gas contained in air, there is a constant balance between the C-14 atoms which have disintegrated and the newly created ones. There are, however, other atom combinations in which this is not the case. With the help of the sun, plants gain nourishment by absorbing carbon dioxide from the air. In so doing they store the carbon dioxide atoms in their leaves and stems. In the chain of the biological process of providing nourishment these same atoms enter the bodies of plant-eating and later of meat-eating animals. But plants and animals can only absorb new carbon while they are still alive. The balance, therefore, between the radio-active C-14 atoms and the normal C-12 atoms must, after their death, slowly shift in favour of C-12 atoms. In time the C-14 atoms disintegrate and the new carbon does not enter the dead body. In 5,730 years half the original amount of C-14 disintegrates. In twice that period of time, i.e. in 11,460 years, only a quarter of the amount remains and so on.

If by means of nuclear technique the relationship of C-14 atoms to C-12 atoms in an early find of bones, for example, can be established, then it is not difficult to calculate the age of the find. Suppose that in an old bone of a reindeer, for every C-12 atom there are found only half as many C-14 atoms as in the carbon dioxide gas contained in the air, then the bone must be exactly 5,730 years old. At the same time it is not too difficult to measure the proportion of the different atoms since C-14 is of course radio-active, and reveals its quantity according to the intensity of its radiation. The tremendous importance which scientists attach to the C-14 process as an accurate 'long-range' clock in their research into prehistory was evidenced in the 1960 award of the Nobel Prize to the physicist Dr. Willard F. Libby for his discovery. For the first time a way had been found of accurately giving the age of finds made of organic material such as bones, wood and charcoal, textiles, ivory and even iron. Iron is not an organic substance, but our forefathers melted it in a charcoal fire in order to work on it. In most cases it suffices to find the smallest particles of coal in a finished tool to be able to gauge the amount of C-14.

But though the Carbon-14 process is of great value it has its limitations. In the first place it is limited to organic material (stalactites are the exception as they take in carbon direct from the air like all growing, living creatures). Secondly the method does not make it possible to give an accurate date to very ancient finds. Its reliability does not extend beyond 50,000 years, but this is quite sufficient for researches into our ancestors who lived after Neanderthal man.

However, there are other modern, though less popular, methods of determining the age of objects. The Thermo-luminescent process was one of the more interesting methods first used in 1960 by the American scholar George C. Kennedy. This method makes it possible to give a date also to non-organic materials. It is easier to explain the principle than it is to put it into practice, as it requires the most careful work. It starts from the premise that radio-active rays cause damage. The radiation destroys the atomic structure of materials which are electrically insulating. The process is similar to the tension of a spring. The greater the tension that is put onto a spring, the greater is the energy which it stores. The same applies to the damage caused by the radio-active rays. The longer the material is subjected to the radiation the greater is the energy which it stores. The likening to the spring is valid in yet another respect. High temperatures repair the damage caused by the radiation. In the process, the energy which has been stored up is again lost. It is diffused in a flash of light.

If a material could be discovered which can conclusively be shown not to have stored any radio-active energy, but in the course of centuries was 'charged' from the continuous cosmic radiation which exists in the universe and the radio-active substances in the earth surrounding it, then this material would act as a timepiece for nuclear physics. Such substances do exist and are in fact frequently found during archaeological excavations. They are clay fragments. In firing the original clay, our forebears unwittingly put the clock back to zero hour for the fragments. The high temperatures used actually extinguished all traces of the rays which had been stored up over tens of thousands of years. The process of storing energy started up again immediately after the firing – the atom clock began to tick. In order to be able to date it from today, the scientist has to be able to answer three questions:

1   How much radiation has penetrated the clay object since the 'clock' was started? (What power was it that pulled the spring?) This can be established by measuring the existing radio-activity at the site of the find.

2   How much energy has the object stored between zero hour and the present day? The answer to this can be found in heating the object. The energy which escapes appears in the form of small flashes of light. Sensitive electronic apparatus is able to register their intensity.

3   How much energy does the object of the find store when subjected to a given dose of radiation? This is shown by the following experiment: After measurement 2 has been applied the object is exposed for a given period to an artificial and accurately measured source of rays. At the same time the experiment establishes the exact amount of energy stored by a renewed application of heat.

A very simple formula allows the age of the fragments to be established in the light of the three measurements which have been recorded.

The few methods mentioned above are quoted to show the skilful way in which scientifically trained investigators of prehistory solve their 'cases'. There are a host of other processes, equally exciting, many of which are still in their infancy. The heyday of the 'legal experts' in the field of archaeology has only just begun.

Atomic science can do much for archaeology but it still cannot evaluate every clue. Nowadays the evidence of doctors, traffic experts, psychologists and members of many other professions is often required to establish or complete the picture in court proceedings. In the same way modern archaeology relies on the expertise of scientists in many different departments.

In 1973 the proceedings of an Austrian society for the study of prehistory contained the following statement: 'Recent research in the Institute of Hygiene of the University of Vienna has shown that many miners working in the Bronze Age salt mines, in Hallein and Hallstadt, suffered from an epidemic of worms. Many miners could only carry on their work suffering greatly from abdominal pain resulting in physical exhaustion. Traces of excrement which had been in existence for 2,500 years contained hundreds of eggs of the whip worm (*trichocephalus dispar*) and the round maw worm (*ascaris limbricoides*). This find gave an insight into the conditions of hygiene in which these men worked.'

The following statement appeared in yet another publication of the same year: 'We must not ignore the value of methods used in the natural sciences. For example, a geologist when examining rock paintings depicting mammals will look into the nature of the material used and on occasion the style dictated by the surface of the rock. The paintings are then reproduced exactly and analysed by zoologists and when possible by animal breeders.'

For some years now, astronomers, with all the scientific skill available to them, have been investigating sun and moon temples which are many thousands of years old, in an attempt to shed some light on their social significance. Surveyors and statisticians versed in the theory of probability are available to give their assistance, supported in many cases by computer establishments. More will be mentioned later in this book about the exciting results of their work. Physicists and chemists are undertaking hundreds of experiments on the materials which have been found. From the scantiest of clues, climatologists are reconstructing the influence of the weather in prehistoric times on the mode of living of our ancestors. Sociologists, ethnologists, theologians and art historians, as well as experts in linguistics and behaviourists, are succeeding in their efforts to obtain insight into the social structure of prehistoric communities. Experts in speleology and ocean-ography are opening up hitherto inaccessible sites where archaeological investigations can be made. Experts in elec-tronics have developed special apparatus to detect objects made of bronze and iron, and an ultra-violet lamp which makes it possible to distinguish old cave paintings which cannot be seen by normal light. Even aviation is making its contribution to modern research into prehistory. An aerial view of interesting archaeological sites often makes it more possible to establish scientific connections than does work on the ground.

From all this, it is clear that research into prehistory is no longer the prerogative of a few specialists. Today many more people are interested in discovering the spiritual and cultural roots of our civilization than the handful of prehistorians who were active at the beginning of the century. This general interest has been extremely beneficial. It has led to exemplary co-operation between the most disparate areas of science. So far this co-operation has been lacking in the work of other researchers such as town planners, doctors and environmentalists, who are far closer to the real world. Without the contributions from all branches of science the world over, it would not have been possible to decipher even a fragment of the traces from prehistory which are the subject of this book. The reader will do well to remember this when, as he reads the various chapters, he asks himself, how is it possible to be so certain about these things? Scientific detection requires a careful reconstruction of events long since past. Every clue, however ambiguous and seemingly unimportant, must be followed up. This is often a very tedious process. Sometimes a step forward is only based on the faintest suspicion, which then has to be either proved or disproved by meticulous and time-consuming work. However, suspense and expectation keep alive the will to work, the reward of which is to be found in the thousand surprises met with and the fresh pieces of knowledge which are acquired.

ART BORN
IN DARKNESS

'Look, Papa, Bulls!'

The cave of Chaffaud near Savigné, in the present département of Vienne was the site of a most remarkable find, for it
was there, in 1840, that the French notary and amateur
speleologist Brouillet discovered a piece of bone with the
design of two stags carved on it. Nothing like it had ever been
seen before. The scholars of prehistory were faced with a
riddle. There was no doubt about the antiquity of the object.
The assumption that it was the work of the Celts seemed
plausible as there was no other earlier civilization to which it
could reasonably have belonged. The riddle remained unsolved and the object was sent to a museum, in fact to the
museum of the town of Cluny. At approximately the same
time two other Frenchmen, Taillefer and Mayor, made an
equally strange find in the cave of Le Veyrier, near Geneva.
The source of this find also remained a mystery and also
created very little stir. Twenty years later, when these ancient
objects were almost forgotten, Alfred Fontan and the 59-year-
old lawyer Edouard Lartet made a sensational discovery in
Massat in the present-day département of Ariège. In the
course of their excavations, in a completely untouched layer of
earth, they came across the bones of animals, long since
extinct, and of a large fragment from the antlers of a stag. On
the antler, clearly recognizable with deep cut lines was
chiselled the head of a bear. In this same layer Lartet found
tools made of stone. All this was certainly no relic of the Celts,
for the animals with which these people lived were animals of
the Ice Age!

Only a few months after this sensational find, at the
beginning of 1861 the first picture of a work of art from the
Ice Age was published in the scientific journal *Annales des
Sciences*. This was the signal in France to begin excavations
with a view to clarifying the problem. In the same year
Alphonse Milne-Edwards undertook a thorough investigation into the Grotto of Lourdes where three years before
Bernadette Soubirous, the daughter of a miller, had had
eighteen visions of the Holy Virgin. Here he discovered a
large number of works of art from the Ice Age. For tens of
thousands of years the cave had been a sacred place! In 1862
Lartet began to dig in the cave of Bruniquel in the present-day
département of Tarn-et-Garonne, a work which was soon
after to be successfully continued by the owner of the land,
Vicomte de Lastic-Saint-Jal.

However, in spite of the number of pieces which had been
discovered in the meantime and in spite of the clear proof
which supported the theory that these works of art dated from

the Ice Age, the professionals remained sceptical. On 8th July 1865 Monsieur Longpierre, director of the collection of antiquities at the Louvre, replied to an offer from the Vicomte de Lastic to give his finds to the famous Paris museum by saying:

'The finds are too uncertain. Until now nothing similar has been discovered in Egypt, Phoenicia and Greece and it is unlikely that there were artists alive in France at the time when an animal world existed which is today extinct. It is all too long ago, and it is impossible to believe that the people of a long past epoch had been as capable of drawing as are the French people of historic times.'

It was not long, however, before there was scientific proof of the authenticity of small finds of the Ice Age. In fact, it was just before Monsieur Longpierre wrote this sceptical letter. In 1864 Lartet and his collaborator, Henry Christy, discovered a bone of a mammoth in the cave of La Madeleine near Les Eyzies-de-Tayac in the Dordogne. On it a human hand had engraved the picture of a mammoth. There was no longer any doubt. Man must have lived at the same time as the huge animal which is now extinct. There were three pieces of evidence to prove that the engraving was neither from a later period nor a fake: carving onto fresh bone leaves smooth edges; old bones splinter. The contours of the mammoth in the cave of La Madeleine were smooth; only a contemporary could have reproduced this animal, for when this object was found in the 19th century, no-one knew what a mammoth actually looked like; furthermore Lartet had once again excavated this bone from a completely untouched layer of earth.

But the triumph of this discovery was not to last long. In 1873 an assistant of the Swiss professor K. Merk substituted some forgeries in the excavations which the professor in good faith stated publicly to be genuine. But when the director of the Museum of Mainz, Ludwig Lindenschmit, shortly afterwards detected the forgeries an avalanche started which could not be stopped and which destroyed the careful work of a decade. Lindenschmit put forward the same arguments as his colleague from the Louvre had done long ago. He declared that it was inconceivable and contradicted any logical theory of the development of art that a man from the Ice Age could have executed such a skilfully-shaped piece of work.

This statement reflected exactly the artistic understanding of the time. It is not surprising that it received a warm welcome from other scholars. In 1877 the participants at a conference of experts in Constance unanimously declared all the works of art from the Ice Age which had so far been discovered to be forgeries. This scholastic theory which had been dignified as a doctrine could not be shaken at the 1878 World Exhibition in Paris, at which some most interesting pieces were exhibited by a few undeterred supporters of the genuineness of the finds of the Ice Age.

Among the visitors to the great Paris Exhibition a Spanish Count, Don Marcelino de Sautuola, took a particular interest in the controversial engraved bones. Some ten years earlier one of his hunting friends in pursuit of a fox had by chance discovered a cave on his land. Was it possible that this cave could also contain artefacts from the Ice Age? The Count left Paris for his home in Santillana del Mar near Torrelavega in northern Spain, and it took him a year before he began to work on this project. But it was not possible to enter the cave since the entrance had been blocked up immediately after its discovery. In the end the Count's curiosity got the better of him and he had the entrance cleared.

What followed sounds like a fairy tale: Don Marcelino began to look around and found the same kind of tools made of stone and bone as he had seen in Paris. This was not all. On one occasion the Count took his four-year-old daughter into

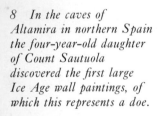

8   In the caves of Altamira in northern Spain the four-year-old daughter of Count Sautuola discovered the first large Ice Age wall paintings, of which this represents a doe.

the cave. The child looked up at the walls and ceiling of the cave by chance and called out: 'Look Papa, bulls!' The little girl had come upon one of the great works of art of the Ice Age in the beam of light given out by the lamp: bison, horses, a female deer, and a wild boar in shades of deep black, fiery red and ochre emerged out of the darkness of the cave. Not far from the entrance to the left, a surface measuring 9 × 18 metres of the wall had been covered with paintings. Some of the animal figures, from 1.2 to 1.9 metres in height, had been carved into the rock, and others had been so skilfully incorporated into the natural rock formations that through the shadow play they almost came alive in the flickering light (see ill. 8 and 9). Was it all a dream or had primitive man really created these elaborate wall paintings? The Count was doubtful. But he could not let the matter drop now. A friend of his, who was a geologist, Professor Vilanova from Madrid, was asked to come to his rescue. The Professor carefully examined the layers of earth in the cave and came to the same conclusion that the paintings were very old and must certainly date from the Ice Age.

Vilanova wrote articles about the fascinating find, lectured on it at the University of Santander and gave the press complete information about it. Excited by the sensational discovery the Spanish people flocked to see the mysterious and

9 'Look Papa, bulls,' called out the excited little girl as she saw the picture of a powerful bison on the cave walls.

gigantic pictures for themselves. Even King Alfonso XII travelled to Santillana del Mar to admire the paintings of Altamira, by which name the cave was known.

Still the experts kept a stony silence. They did not try to produce counter evidence, they simply ignored Altamira on the grounds that what should not exist does not exist. At a large international Congress on prehistorical archaeology held in Lisbon in 1880, and attended by all the leading experts of Europe, the Altamira cave was only mentioned on one occasion, and that was when Vilanova issued an invitation to the scholars to go and see the paintings for themselves. However, the experts clearly regarded it as beneath their dignity to embark on an excursion to a place which was clearly exploited by charlatans. Professor Vilanova was not even given the opportunity to report on the paintings at the meeting.

The idea that complete works of art had already existed long before the Greek and Roman classical periods was as inconceivable at that time as was, at an earlier date, Galileo's theory that the earth revolved round the sun, when, according to the generally held belief, the earth was the centre of the universe.

The experts' unanimous rejection of Altamira dealt a blow to research into the Ice Age from which it did not recover for two decades. Nine years after the disastrous Congress of Lisbon in 1889 the French archaeologist Léopold Chiron reported in provincial newspapers and in several scientific journals that two years earlier he had also discovered drawings of men and animals in the Chabot Cave near Aiguèze. His publications also failed to arouse any interest.

In the following years speleologists and archaeologists in France discovered four more caves with paintings and engravings from the Ice Age. But none of them had the courage to publish their finds for fear of appearing ridiculous. This is the reason why the caves of Teyjat in the Dordogne (discovered 1889), La Mouthe near Les Eyzies-de-Tayac (discovered 1895), Pair-non-Pair in the Gironde (discovered 1896) and Marsoulas in the département of Haute-Garonne (discovered 1897) remained unknown until the turn of the century; and today La Mouthe and Pair-non-Pair are reckoned to be among the most important art treasures in Europe.

A Sceptic Admits His Mistake

A little more than 100 kilometres to the east of the port of Bordeaux in the bend of the little mountain river Vézère lies a small, sleepy place, Les Eyzies-de-Tayac. Vertical chalk cliffs tower picturesquely over forests of holm-oak trees and groups of large juniper bushes, or stretch along the river like a wall, 50 metres or more in height. In other places the river winds lazily through meadows and fields. Both banks of the river are bordered with tall poplar trees. On 8th September 1901 three young men, Dr. Capitan, the village school-teacher Monsieur Peyrony, and the 24-year-old Abbé Breuil set out from Les Eyzies-de-Tayac on an expedition following not the Vézère but a small stream, the Beune, which flows into the Vézère at Les Eyzies. Their route took them eastwards in the direction of the hamlet Girouteaux. After about half an hour they reached Berniche, an isolated farm at the end of the valley of Combarelles. The farmhouse lay close to the wall of a cliff with a stable built into the rock. The three young men exchanged a few words with the farmer and quite by chance their conversation touched on prehistory. For the inhabitants of the valley this was quite a common topic of conversation. A few years earlier a young man from Les Eyzies had discovered the cave paintings of La Mouthe on the land of a farm 2 kms to the south of Les Eyzies. This discovery occurred when the farmer wanted to extend his barn and knocked a hole into the back wall. The young man had walked through this hole to find himself in a cave. 'If you are interested,' said the farmer of Berniche to the three young men, 'I know of similar pictures.' When asked where these were he answered, 'On our land there are stalactites and pictures of animals.' The young doctor, the teacher and the priest did not hesitate. They followed the farmer into an underground cattle-shed which was connected to a huge grotto. They jumped over the chicken roost and found themselves in a narrow passage almost 6 metres high which led 100 metres into the mountain. By the light of their lamps they discovered deep-cut engravings on the walls which were gradually recognized to be of reindeer, horses and mammoths. There were many figures drawn on top of each other which the young scholars were only able to make out later. They depicted bears, wild cats and even a rhinoceros.

Only four days after the discovery of Combarelles, Denis Peyrony, the teacher, wrote the following letter to his friend, the Abbé Henri Breuil, who in the meantime had left Les Eyzies:

'I have just found today in another cave, paintings of perfect beauty though they are slightly disfigured by inscriptions which visitors have made. There are also some engravings but these are not as deeply cut as those at Combarelles. I am writing to Dr. Capitan about this. If he is unable to return I should be very glad if you would sacrifice some of your holiday as I am in fact now doing.'

Three days later the Abbé Breuil and Dr. Capitan were both back in Les Eyzies. They were enthusiastic about the paintings. As he later wrote in a provincial paper, the Abbé Breuil felt deep inside himself a vocation to devote himself to the study of prehistory which was to remain with him for life. When at the age of 17 he was studying at the Seminar of Issy, his instructor had said to him almost prophetically: 'There is much to be done in the study of prehistory and you should devote yourself to it.' He was proved right. The priest was determined to put all his energy into breaking the 20-year-old ban imposed by the disastrous Congress of Lisbon which hung like a curse of arrogant witch-doctors over the art of the Ice Age. Incontestable proof had to be found for the authenticity of the cave paintings. The engravings in Combarelles would not provide this but the paintings in the newly discovered cave of Font-de-Gaume could well do so. Some of the paintings were covered with a stalactitic formation which in places was 2 centimetres thick. This should have convinced the experts of their great age. But the Abbé and his two colleagues wanted to be completely certain. They asked Professor Henri Moissan, who was to be awarded the 1906 Chemistry Nobel Prize, to undertake an analysis of the colours of the paintings at his institute.

From that day on it was smooth going. Only eleven days after the discovery of Font-de-Gaume Professor Moissan read a paper at the Academy of Sciences entitled *A newly discovered cave with wall paintings of figures from palaeolithic* times*.

* The Old Stone Age which falls within the Ice Age.

'The cave of Font-de-Gaume faces west and lies half way up a chalk cliff on the road from Les Eyzies to Saint-Cyprien, some 20 metres above the valley. Its shape is that of a long tube about 123.8 metres in length with three irregular extensions of 15 metres, 21 metres and 48 metres respectively. The width of the cave varies in diameter between 2 and 3 metres in some places and 7 to 8 metres in others. In some places it becomes little more than a narrow passage.

'The first four paintings begin 65.7 metres from the entrance to the cave immediately after a very narrow passage which opens up 1.7 metres above ground level in the middle of a wall of stalagmites.'

'Nearly all these pictures,' wrote the professor, 'have been painted with very fine brush strokes which are emphasized by a 1 to 2 centimetres wide black border surrounding the entire animal. Frequently some part of the animal, the paws for example, is painted entirely in this black colour. Some animals like the large deer (1.5 metres in length) or a little wild horse (0.5 metres long) are painted entirely in black. They form silhouettes in the same way as primitive Greek painting on vases. Sometimes the brush stroke is drawn in black and sometimes in red ochre. In this case the brush stroke is very broad. But in most cases the main surface of the animals is painted completely with red ochre surrounded by a black line. Sometimes certain parts such as the head of the wild ox appear to be painted in red and black which results in a browny colour. On the other hand, in the case of many animals the head is black and the rear is painted in a browny colour. This total in-colouring, which resembles genuine fresco painting, was often applied over the engraved outline of the animal. In other cases some of the paint had been actually scraped away after its application. Finally the contours were underlined by a definite scratching away of the surface outside the edge of the painting. This recalls the method used in wood-carving to bring out prominent areas. In some cases the artist used the natural bumps in the stone to emphasize definite parts of the animal. Many of the figures (decorated by flutings or in colour) are covered with a stalactitic overlay which can be as much as 2 centimetres thick.

'The figures continue to the bottom of the cave which ends in a narrow passage. Some of them are almost near the ground and others 4 metres up. Some of the animals are 2.5 metres in length, as, for example, a large wild ox painted entirely in red. Many animals are over 1 metre long and others measure only 0.5 metres. In general they are very large.' The professor then continued to describe the various subject matters of the 77 paintings: wild oxen, reindeer, deer, wild horses, antelopes, mammoths and geometrical signs.

In a subsequent publication written for the Academy of Sciences, Henri Moissan went into great detail on the conclusions drawn from his thorough analyses of the colours. He ended decisively: 'In conclusion it can be said that the colours used for the paintings in the cave of Font-de-Gaume were ochre derived from iron and manganese oxides.'

Some time later archaeologists in the Font-de-Gaume excavations found implements and stores of paints which had been used by the Ice Age artists: stone scorers and blades, engraver's chisels and other utensils as well as pieces of ochre, some of which were egg-shaped and others three-cornered, and crayons of manganic oxide mixed with clay. Similar 'studio apparatus' was found in other caves.

This made it possible for the experts to reconstruct their drawing and painting techniques. The artists of the Stone Age first sketched the outlines with the black manganic crayons. In stone mortars they broke up the more crumbly red iron oxide colours and stirred them with water or fish oil. They applied this liquid mixture with brushes made of animal hair fitted into hollow bone tubes, or dabs. They even knew and used the modern 'spray technique'. The dry colour powder was easily blown through wooden or bone tubes onto the wet walls of the caves. The peculiar quality of the water in the caves was responsible for the fact that paints which were not soluble in water stuck to the walls and survived for tens of thousands of years. This water contained dissolved chalk. When the Ice Age painters applied their paints to the wet walls of the caves, the dampness penetrated the layer of colour. In the course of time the water evaporated and the chalk which had been dissolved hardened into a solid film which permanently united the particles of paint with the wall. Professor Moissan's convincing and scientifically documented lectures and publications had with a single blow made the Ice Age paintings respectable. There was no longer any doubt that this accomplished form of art was the work of prehistoric artists. After being rejected for 20 years it was now treated with enthusiasm. Abbé Breuil himself managed to convert one of the strongest earlier critics, the archaeologist Emile Cartailhac of the University of Toulouse. In September 1902 they visited together the almost forgotten cave of Altamira. Cartailhac was fascinated. From there he wrote to a friend: 'We should be so happy if you could be here with us. Altamira is the most beautiful, the strangest and the most exciting of all caves with mural paintings.* The Abbé has been making sketches of the bison, horses, deer and wild boar, the colours of which are quite perfect.'

Cartailhac's feelings were a mixture of enthusiasm and shame. Ashamed because for 20 years he had been one of the bitter opponents of Altamira. But he was so enthralled with all that this fantastic new world revealed to him that he was glad to admit his mistake publicly. His article: *La Grotte d'Altamira. Mea culpa d'un sceptique* (*The Cave of Altamira. Mea culpa of a sceptic*) became known all over the world. In this article Cartailhac admits to being among those guilty of a great scientific injustice. Even the famous explorer Martillet had endorsed his beliefs at that time. In a letter sent to Cartailhac's home he had written: 'Be on your guard! A trick is about to be played on French prehistory scholars. Beware of the traps set by Spanish clerics.' Cartailhac frankly admits: 'I

* The famous French Lascaux caves had not yet been discovered.

listened to this warning, which led to this dreadful error. After
the discoveries in the Dordogne of the caves with paintings
nothing justified further doubts about the age of the Altamira
cave . . . In our youth, we thought that we knew all the
answers, but the discoveries of Abbé Breuil and others and the
wonderful finds and collections of works of art in Piette prove
that our scientific pursuits, like other scientific pursuits, tell
an unending story which will continue to unfold.'

400 Centuries of Art

Ever since 1901, when the trio Breuil, Peyrony and Dr.
Capitan discovered the caves of Combarelles and Font-de-
Gaume, the continual series of finds of Ice Age paintings has
never ceased. In France alone today there are 77 known caves
and rock-formations engraved with works of art dating from
the Old Stone Age. In Spain there are 46. Southern Italy has
four finds and Germany one (near Kelheim, where there is an
engraving of an ibex). Recently scholars engaged in research
have discovered Ice Age cave paintings both in Portugal
(1964, near Escoural) and in Russia (1961, the Kapova cave in
the southern Urals). (The more important of the 130 finds are
shown in Map 1 on page 261.) Most of them are now closed to
tourists.

Altogether the European caves of the Ice Age contain 4,000
individual paintings. There are figures of horses, goats,
mammoths, bison and ibex, oxen and other wild cattle, wild
boar, rhinoceros, bears, lions, fishes, birds, imaginary creatures and also human beings. Sometimes individual hands are
depicted, sometimes stylized female bodies are drawn with
pronounced sexual organs. And now and then mysterious
symbolic designs, especially the 'Tectiform' signs (long-
drawn-out, three-cornered wedges) are to be found in many of
the caves.

The paintings in nearly every one of the important caves
have their own special characteristics. And yet certain
similarities exist among them. Common characteristics
denote the different periods in style to which they belonged.
Abbé Breuil, who conscientiously copied hundreds of these
figures and carefully studied their lines and colourings, had
already distinguished in 1906 four periods which succeeded
each other. Six years later he subdivided the first of these
periods into two. Breuil's general description of the development of art in the Ice Age was as follows: Art in the Old Stone
Age can be said to have developed in two big cycles; the first
one, the Aurignacian-Perigordian period, lasted from about
30,000 or even 40,000 to 20,000 B.C., the second one, the

10   The caves of Bara-Bahau near Les Eyzies-de-Tayac in the Dordogne claim to be the cradle of art. Many scholars estimate that this hand scored into the rock is nearly 40,000 years old.

Solutrean-Magdalenian period, followed immediately, and lasted for about 10,000 years. The first cycle began with simple patterns and drawings of the outlines only, first of the human hand, and subsequently of animals (see ill. 10 and 11). Later, according to Breuil's theory, the Aurignacian artists painted the animals using one and sometimes two colours. In the beginning of the second cycle during the Solutrean period (about 19,000 to 18,000 B.C.) there followed a kind of lull in artistic creation until the Magdalenian period, when something like a renaissance in cave paintings began. Again this began with clean, simple outlines, at first making faint lines which later became firmer, almost as though drawn with a thick paste, and only later these lines became delicate and free. Again the artist began by enlivening the centre of the figures by partially painting them and dabbing them with red and blue dots. In their final multi-coloured form these wall paintings were extremely expressive.

Abbé Breuil's analysis of the styles of painting during the Ice Age was generally accepted for decades, and from time to time it is restated in new publications on the subject. But the 'Father of prehistory', as archaeologists sometimes refer to Abbé Breuil, was mistaken. It is an irony of historical research: 25 years earlier in 1901, Breuil and his friend had completely reversed expert opinion by proving the authenticity of the Ice Age paintings in Font-de-Gaume, and by 1926 it was proving equally difficult for him to see beyond his own theories. Breuil's thought processes had their origins in

the 19th century. At that time it was considered that there was
only one line of development in the arts, from the picturesque
to a more elaborate colourful painting. The idea that artists
could change their technique to a simpler, more stylised
method, less flowing, but nevertheless more assertive, was
alien to them. These were the blinkers with which Breuil and
another, almost equally important scholar of the Ice Age,
Hugo Obermaier, viewed the art of the Old Stone Age. As
those were the only ones known to them, both learned men
applied the artistic standards of the late 19th century to the
cave paintings. In the autumn of 1940 Abbé Breuil's theory of
style was put to the test. Four young boys from the village of
Montignac, which like Les Eyzies is on the river Vézère, while
searching for their dog lost in the wood, quite by chance
discovered the cave of Lascaux. This is one of the most
impressive and important caves dating from the Ice Age.
Breuil, who was immediately called in by the village school-
master, suddenly found himself in front of some 800
beautifully preserved images on the ceiling and walls of this
cave, images which had been hidden in darkness for
thousands of years. Here were engravings with movement,
fine animal paintings in black, yellow, red and brown (see ill.
12 and 13); vigorously drawn massive bulls amidst wild,
galloping horses, and immediately next to this a peaceful little
group of stags. In front of all these animals stands a strange
creature of the long forgotten past, the 'Licorne', the

*11   The animals which
our ancestors engraved onto
the walls of the cave of
Bara-Bahau were Ice Age
animals: bison, lions,
Aurochs and wild horses.*

12   More than a hundred generations drew and painted sacred pictures on the walls of caves of the Grotto of Lascaux. Wild horses decorating the 'Hall of Oxen' date from between 20,000 and 15,000 B.C. The pictures of the two prehistoric bullocks painted in outline are more recent; they probably date from between 13,000 and 10,000 B.C.

13   In the innermost recesses of the caves of Lascaux, in the 'pit', there is the famous scene of the 'socerer'.

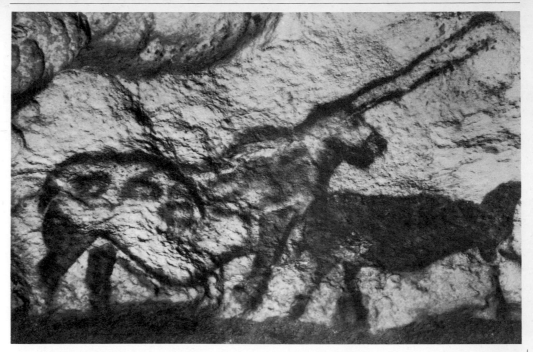

14 *The 'Unicorn' of Lascaux posed many problems. Dr. Kurt Turnovsky of Vienna has recently put forward the idea that this might have been the* Elasmotherium sibiricum, *a rhinoceros–like animal which lived during the Ice Age.*

15 *The swimming stags of Lascaux (15,000 to 10,000 B.C.) belong to the most recent Ice Age wall paintings.*

mysterious unicorn of Lascaux (see ill. 14). In the other halls
and passages of the cave various animals seem to be actually
moving as they follow the natural contours of the walls: a
leaping cow with a long neck, a rearing horse, stags swimming
(see ill. 15), charging oxen, fiercely galloping archaic bulls.
And here and there hunting scenes, feathered arrows darting
past and strange designs which many scholars think represent
snares.

To which period of art of the Ice Age do these Lascaux
masterpieces belong? The animals which they depict give us
some guidelines. In contrast to other caves, there are no
paintings of mammoths and also no bison. Except for one
drawing of a reindeer and a single rhinoceros there are no
other animals typical of the Ice Age. This could mean one of
three things: the paintings could either date from the period at
the very beginning of the Ice Age when the climate was mild
(the early Aurignacian-Perigordian period) or from one of
the centuries immediately after the Ice Age, i.e. from the
Magdalenian period. The third possibility would be the
period towards the end of the Aurignacian-Perigordian cycle,
a time when, in the middle of the last period of the Ice Age, the
climate in Europe became temporarily milder. This would
mean that in round figures the Lascaux paintings are either
30,000 or 12,000 to 15,000 years old or, according to the third
theory, they are 24,000 years old and therefore just half-way
between the other two periods.

The first estimate can be definitely ruled out, as it is clear
from the Lascaux paintings that they could not have been
done at the beginning of an artistic period which continued its
development for another 1,000 years. The fact that there were
hardly any reindeer portrayed in the cave speaks for the
theory that the paintings could be 12–15,000 years old,
because 15,000 years ago these animals no longer existed in
the wild in central Europe, whereas 24,000 years ago they
were still quite common. Breuil and Obermaier were nevertheless convinced, because of their style, that these paintings
originated well before the end of the Ice Age, and clung to the
belief that they were 24,000 years old. Even later, when the
newly developed C-14 method proved that the Lascaux caves
were 15,516 years old (with an error of at most 900 years either
way) the then 75-year-old Abbé refused to be convinced.

Meanwhile a professor of prehistory from Mainz, Herbert
Kühn, had worked out a different interpretation, based on
stylistic evidence. When Kühn began researching the Ice Age,
he was not hampered by 19th century preconceptions on the
history of art. At the age of 23, in 1918, he had been awarded a

doctorate at the University of Jena for his thesis on the psychological foundations of modern art. What Breuil had thought to be impossible he knew to be an actual fact: the representational style was not the culmination of all artistic development. Art can develop beyond it and then, developing through a stylized period, move on to the abstract. The representative becomes the symbolic. Why then shouldn't a similar development have begun towards the end of the Ice Age?

When Kühn put forward his new theory of style in the Ice Age art, he was aware that he was deviating from the generally accepted scholarly view. He wrote: 'The interpretation of the development of style which I propose differs greatly from that which the great expert in the art of the Ice Age Henri Breuil (1877–1961) had expounded on many occasions.' In a few short sentences Kühn outlined the result of his research:

'The succession of the movements in style is clearly illustrated in three different sets of pictures. The paintings of Aurignac reveal a firm and clearly defined linear style (ill. 16).

'The paintings of the Solutrean and the middle Magdalenian period depict a pictorial and plastic style.

'In the paintings of the late Magdalenian period we find a linear style again, but one that is more developed and subtler than that of the Aurignac paintings. I would like to charac-

16 The earliest cave pictures (30,000, perhaps 40,000 B.C.), are nothing more than outlines. During that period the legs of animals are often found to be missing. (Bara-Bahau near Les Eyzies-de-Tayac.)

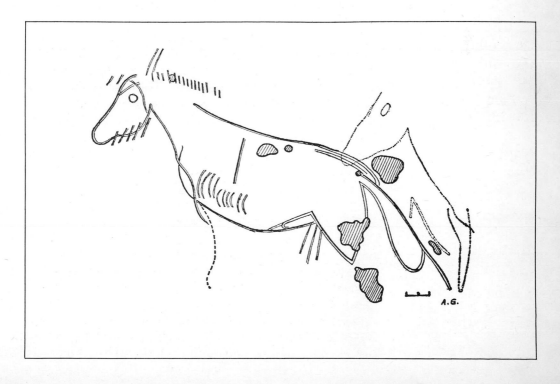

terize it as the "swinging style"' (see ill. 12: deer).

'A close friendship bound me to the two scholars Breuil and Obermaier,' wrote Kühn in another place. 'I discussed these ideas with them on many occasions. But they did not follow me. They regarded the pictorial style, as depicted in Altamira and Niaux, as the end of the Ice Age. In that case there would be no progression to the abstract art of the Old Stone Age; the necessary connecting link to the new linear style of the late Magdalenian period, which I call the swinging style, is missing. Without this connecting link many paintings would be wrongly dated, perhaps even those of Lascaux.'

Professor Kühn's conclusions were supported by the dates established by repeated Carbon 14 process testings. They were also confirmed by a number of documented small finds which were executed in a style similar to the wall paintings, the dates of which could be determined with certainty. Art had changed during the period of the Ice Age. The 'visual' picture evolved out of the 'tactile' picture, to use Professor Kühn's expression. The 'tactile' picture extracts the character of the animal which is being portrayed, with its firmly outlined contours and later with its spread of colour covering the whole surface. The 'visual' picture reproduces freely the object which is being observed, and is not restricted by any set forms. It depicts the fighting bull, the jumping deer, just as they appear to the hunter in a split second. Out of the fixed timelessness of the style of the Aurignacian period there evolves in the style of the later Magdalenian period, the instant snapshot of movement.

The Dance of the Magicians
In the valley of the Vézère near Les Eyzies, anyone who digs the foundations for a house or lays out a new path, or works a trench to lay pipes, must be prepared to suddenly find himself dropped in the middle of the drama of the Old Stone Age.

This is what happened in 1868 to some railway workers who had to dig up an old country road in the course of the reconstruction of the railway line from Périgueux to Agen. Suddenly their picks struck the vault of a cave. There followed a most macabre discovery; the cave was filled with human bones. They called their foreman, who in turn summoned the contractor. The contractor ordered the workers to suspend their operations and called in a well-known archaeologist, Olaine Laganne. Excavations began and revealed flint tools, animal bones, two human skulls, and six complete skeletons: the bones of an old man, three grown-up men, a young woman and her baby. There was no doubt that

17   The years between 20,000 and 15,000 B.C. are poor in wall paintings. But there is a series of clay and rock carvings from that time, such as these two small clay bison from the Tuc d'Audoubert in the département of Ariège. (The photograph is of a copy in the museum of Les Eyzies-de-Tayac.)

18   These fine high relief carvings of bullocks in the grotto of Bourdeilles in the Dordogne are only 45 cm tall.

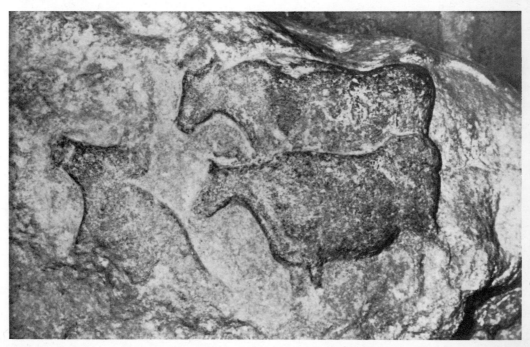

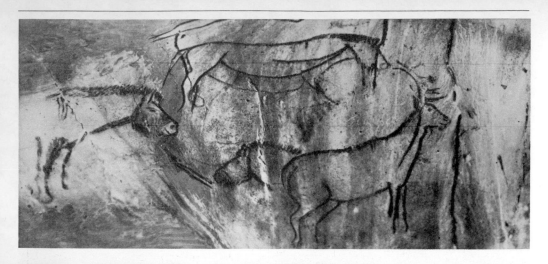

19 One of the most important caves with Ice Age paintings is near Niaux in the south-eastern Pyrenees. The shaggy wild horses are typical of the period.

20 The lightly treated but very graphic style of painting is exemplified by this ibex.

these bones were very old, as one of the skulls was covered with a stalactite formation. Another thing was discovered by the archaeologists. The remains of the woman were witness to a drama tens-of-thousands-of-years-old. Somebody had brutally struck her down. There was a deep cut in the bones of her forehead, and next to her skeleton there was a stone mallet, which fitted exactly into the opening of the wound. Was she the victim of a brutal murder or had some priest of the Ice Age brought her there as a sacrifice? We will never know the truth.

21 *This Ice Age painting of a horse's head in the cave at Rouffignac has a sculptured effect. The artist has used the rounded surface formation to highlight the features of the animal.*

22 *Mammoths are a recurrent theme in the Rouffignac cave paintings.*

However, the outstanding significance of the skeleton find of Cro–Magnon did not lie in the macabre drama of prehistoric murder. It was the first time that scientists had come across the remains of a human race which had lived after Neanderthal man, and the evidence showed that it was the earliest human remains to give evidence of 'Homo Sapiens', the creature endowed with understanding, the precursor of contemporary man. As Cro–Magnon man he took his place in prehistory. It was he who was responsible for the thousands of completed carvings and paintings on the walls and roofs of the Ice Age caves.

But what inspired the men of Cro–Magnon to execute these enormous paintings by the flickering light of a flint or stone oil lamp deep in the recesses of the mountains? Paintings which are often found in passages and corners of caves which are most difficult to enter. Pictures, painted on the walls of narrow crevices, which in many cases cannot be seen in their entirety because there is not sufficient room to stand back. Pictures which the artist could only have painted with difficulty either lying down or with the upper half of his body bending back, or pictures which completely filled up the space of a wall painted close together or even on top of each other, while large areas of the surface of a cave lay untouched all these thousands of years?

Speculation about these riddles has flourished ever since their discovery, and still goes on. The interpretations range

23 *The Vézère valley in the Dordogne is rich in overhanging cliffs, so-called 'Abris' (shelters). This large Abri at Les Eyzies-de-Tayac shelters the museum which is well worth visiting.*

from pure wall decoration to the claim, undoubtedly inspired by the private fantasies of the interpreter, that these bison and deer, bulls and horses, were nothing more than symbols of a powerful sex-cult in which, for example, the wild horse embodied the female and the bison the male element. Many of these theories about the meaning of Ice Age art are easily disproved, others simply have no basis. The theory that they were merely mural decorations is easily refuted, for example, by the fact that the painted sections of the cave were quite certainly uninhabited. They were often to be found several hundred metres into the cave, in nearly inaccessible places, often very narrow and therefore unsuitable for human habitation, and naturally pitch dark.

Furthermore, the remains of fires, domestic implements or other traces of everyday life were never found.

Nowadays most experts are convinced that the large Ice Age paintings and carvings are an expression of the religious feelings of our early ancestors. This is obvious because, in the case of primitive peoples, the origins of art are nearly always to be found in religion, in religious ceremonies. It is just as true of the natives of Africa, the Red Indians of the American continent, the original inhabitants of Japan, as well as the various peoples of the South Seas. It was not very different in the case of the more developed civilizations; Egyptian art was a religious art; the same is no less true of the art of China, of Mesopotamia, of the art of the Mayas and the Incas, of the art of the Arab world, of the art of classical Greece, and later that of the European Middle Ages.

But on its own that fact is no proof that the art of tens of thousands of years ago must have had the same roots. However there are other, more convincing, reasons which support this theory. In the caves the rooms which had mural paintings were hard to reach and were set deep in the inmost recesses of the mountains. They were sacred places, to which, perhaps, only a few chosen members of a sect had access; these · were priests, and magicians who here, far removed from everyday life, performed ritual ceremonies in paintings and in dances, and practised mysterious hunting and fertility rites (see ill. 24). There was never any lack of opponents to this theory, of art historians, who maintained that the well-drawn and lifelike scenes of raging bulls, graceful deer or huge mammoths, could not have been the product of traditional religious painting, but must have been nothing more than the expression of the joy of artistic creation. They based their view on the fact that there was evidence in the Ice Age of well-planned art schools with well-equipped studios for painting.

Their view was not entirely wrong, but is it a fact that an artist's joy in his creation of necessity excludes the possibility that Art could spring from a religious origin?

Two of the leading experts on prehistoric art, Abbé Breuil and Professor Herbert Kühn of Mainz, both of whom devoted their lives to the study of this period of art, expressed the same thoughts. Breuil wrote: 'It has often been debated whether

24 In 1953 Bernabo Bréa discovered Ice Age engravings in the cave of Addaura on Monte Pellegrino near Palermo. The scene portrayed is a ritual dance of magicians.

the art of the Stone Age was the product of the artist's spontaneity, a love of beauty, of art for art's sake . . . or whether the creations did not serve some practical, some magic purpose . . . In reality these two points of view are not contradictory, nor are they mutually exclusive, but they complement each other. No great art can be born, or develop without that artistic temperament which is a passionate enthusiasm for beauty. But without a society which shows a real interest in his creations, the artist cannot live or found schools which will ensure that his technical discoveries and his love of beauty will survive and continue both in place and time.'

And Kühn says:

'The caves are places of worship, temples, the pictures are religious pictures, it is religion which provides the foundation for that art . . . This fact does not mean that the people of this era did not have an artistic sensibility, capability or comprehension. It is a false idea of our contemporaries that it must be either art or religion. Both are closely inter-connected and this interpretation should be self-evident.'

Art as the expression of religious feeling, of the spell of the hunt, and of the cult of fertility, that was the meaning of the great paintings of the Ice Age. 'The magic religious meaning,' Professor Kühn explains, 'results from six facts: firstly from their frequent location in places within the caves which are difficult to get to. Secondly the arrow markings on the pictures of animals. Thirdly the arrow wounds on the animal sculptures or reliefs. Fourthly the traces of dance steps round the sculptures. Fifthly the pictures of magicians with animal masks. Sixthly the great number of pictures in one place, the place of consecration, in the archaeological finds which have now been closed.'

Recently Alexander Marshack has again taken up the old theme of the meaning of Ice Age art. In 1975 in an essay in the popular American scientific journal *The National Geographic Magazine* he wrote about himself. 'I have wandered all over Europe, from Sweden in the north to the south coast of Spain, to the heel of the boot of Italy. I have examined thousands of Ice Age objects and carvings, a great part of which was excavated at the cultural and ritual remains of Cro-Magnon man. I have spent months looking at sketches and have analysed paintings and engravings in the most important caves in Europe.' Marshack worked with such technical and scientific aids as microscopes, infra-red films, and ultra-violet lamps. Many of the results of his work confirm what had already been known; for example he established in

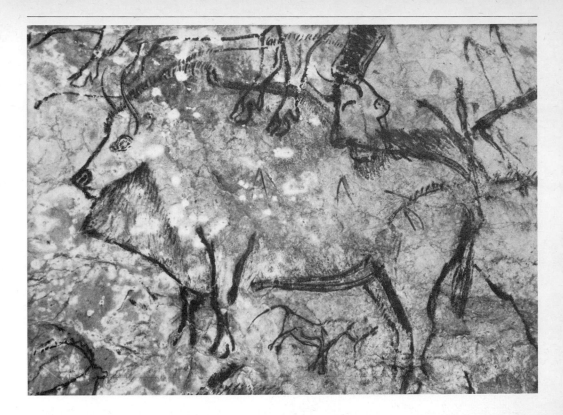

what sequence the paintings and engravings of the Ice Age had been superimposed on each other, and that they used different tools one after another to produce the destructive and often puzzling lines which, in the professional jargon of the scholars of prehistory, are called 'Macaroni'. Marshack's conclusions nowadays seem somewhat speculative, perhaps because these ideas are still too new, too unusual. This scholar interprets the engravings on the bone tools and on the walls of the caves as symbolic representations of spring and autumn, as they break the rhythm of the year. He found sixty-nine signs engraved on a reindeer bone which was 30,000 years old, examined it under a microscope and established that they had been made with twenty-four different tools, and that they had certainly not been made at the same time. Was the bone a three-hundred-year-old moon calendar on which an earlier observer of the heavens daily inscribed the changing shape of the earth's satellite over two-and-a-quarter moon months? The shape of the small incisions, partly in the form of a sickle and partly in the form of a full circle, speak for rather than against this theory.

Marshack deduced from this and from the representation of the seasons the method of calculating time which was used in the Ice Age. In the much scored, stylized, heavy-hipped female torso he claimed to recognize an Ice Age woman's

25   In the cave at Niaux the magic powers of the Ice Age painting to propitiate the spirit and secure a successful hunt are recognized by the arrows with which the magicians slew the bison representing the living beast . . .

*26 ... and also the pit
represented by three
horizontal strokes into
which this mammoth has
fallen as found in the cave
painting at Rouffignac.*

monthly jottings noting her menstrual periods or various phases of her pregnancy. Whether Marshack is right in his interpretations the future will tell, but his investigations have incontestably confirmed one thing; the concern many scholars of the Ice Age have to preserve the rare testimonies of the earliest beginnings of art. Marshack's ultra-violet lamp revealed not only a number of brush strokes which had until then remained undetected but also a thin layer of particles of dust which glittered suspiciously. The dust consisted of tiny blue-green spots and long winding bits of a bright red and blue-green fabric. Under the microscope the dust showed up a mixture of pollen, mushroom and fern spores, and man-made fibres which 20th-century visitors had brought in with them. These spores and specks of pollen are fatal to the Ice Age pictures which had survived for tens of thousands of years in the remoteness of the caves in perpetual darkness and nearly constant temperatures. No less harmful are the air currents caused by the daily visits, and the rise in temperature due to the influx of outside air and the human body heat of the visitors.

Because of the damage these influences caused to the paintings in a number of caves the triple doors of Lascaux were closed to the public. In the previous year 120,000 tourists had visited the cave. Other caves were not opened to conducted tours. In the meantime specialists had removed the

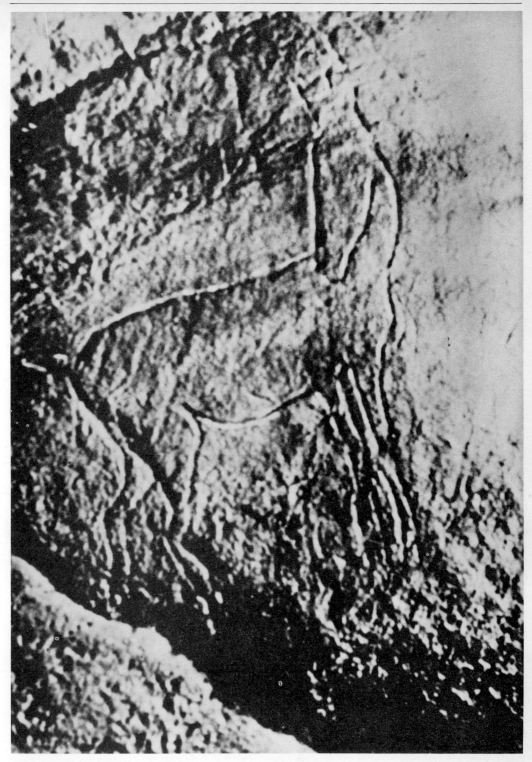

27 *On the little island of Levanzo to the west of Sicily there is a cave with rock carvings dating from the Old and New Stone Ages. This picture of a female stag looking round is one of the oldest, about 13,000 to 10,000 B.C.*

28 The entrance to the cave at Niaux: the enormous opening was the result of a split in the rock caused by frost.

most severe dangers to the paintings in Lascaux, but the caves are still closed to visitors. To compensate for this, interested tourists can go to an information and documentation centre next to the sacred shrine of the Ice Age. They can also visit many other caves, containing paintings of no lesser significance such as Rouffignac, Cougnac, Pech-Merle, Pair-non-Pair, Niaux, and others unnamed, which are the hallowed sites of our earliest ancestors.

ART EMERGES FROM THE DARK

When the Countryside Changed

Anyone who knows someone or has himself once climbed the mighty Matterhorn is aware of how high a thousand metres is, and can realize what a tremendous force of weight the huge bulk of rock exerts on its base. Compared to the vast glaciers which covered the whole of northern Europe, the Matterhorn is small. In places the glaciers were two or three times as big and exerted at least as much pressure on the ground beneath them as the peaks of the Matterhorn. It is no wonder that the land mass changed, as the large areas of ice began to melt some 12,000 years ago, and in the south gradually freed bare stretches of land, which were often covered by mounds of rubble as high as a tower. Soon large stretches of land which had just been uncovered disappeared. They were swallowed up in the rising waters created by the melting snow. The level of the oceans rose a hundred metres and flooded vast areas. Where there was once a continent, now there was a sea. The North Sea and the Baltic Sea, and large parts of the Adriatic sea date from this period. Do the legends of the great flood, which are found in the Bible and elsewhere, recall this world-wide catastrophe? Some serious scholars are convinced that they do.

In the course of time many regions rose out of the water, and, freed from the enormous pressure of the ice, began to breathe again. Gradually they began to rise like a foam rubber cushion after someone has been sitting on it.

All in all, the retreating ice released more land than was swallowed up by the melting waters. Soon life began on the new, fertile land. Tundra grass spread with the first knee-high trees such as the polar willow, the dwarf birch, or the juniper. Later they were joined by groves of mountain ash and clusters of full-sized birch trees; gradually birds and mammals reappeared: the unassuming reindeer, herds of wild horses, various waterfowl, wild geese, ducks and swans. A further reoccurrence of the cold period made many of them, and the taller species of trees, disappear from the countries of northern Europe. At last the climate became warmer. Great forests pushed further and further to the north. Birch trees and pine covered the landscape, and in the damp earth of the extensive lowlands there grew mountain ash, willows, and trembling poplars.

The woods were teeming with wild animals. Deer and elks, wild oxen, brown bears and wild boar made their haunts in the undergrowth. Large stretches of primitive forest were inhabited by hares, beavers, wild cats, foxes, badgers, and hedgehogs. Tall reeds surrounded the many lakes and ponds,

29 *Archaeologists have found 5,000-year-old mounds of 'Kitchen Midden' several metres deep on the coasts of the various islands in present-day Denmark. This pile of oyster shells can be seen at Ertebølle.*

and in summer thousands of yellow and white water-lilies made a fine show on the waters filled with darting pike and perch.

All this was 8,000 years ago. In northern Europe it continued to grow warmer. Hazel trees, oak, elms and lime trees took root in the forests; eventually the oak tree dominated. But oak forests are darker than the copses of pine and birch trees which they had replaced. Oak forests are also damper. They are ill suited to many animals because they kill the undergrowth on which they live. It was during this period that the elk and the wild ox emigrated to the north.

The great transformation in the landscape of northern Europe did not take place in a day. More than two hundred generations of our ancestors lived during this period of transition. As in the Ice Age they were hunters and gatherers, and as big game moved further and further to the north, they followed, bound to them for better or for worse. As the sea worked its way further and further into stretches of land they became more and more familiar with it; they caught its fish, hunted seals and porpoises, and later as the game moved further north they collected shell-fish. That was about 5,000 years ago.

Huge mounds of shellfish shells, particularly of large, magnificent oysters, were the first traces which archaeologists found of human beings of the Late Ice Age. Anyone who has wandered along the Roskilde fjord, the Arresø, the Mariager fjord or Limfjorden in north-east Denmark will have noticed the inland precipices which border the shoreline meadows everywhere. That was the old coast line and the rambler will come across the huge heaps of brilliant white shells dating from the Middle Stone Age (see ill. 29). Many of them are higher than a man, 20 metres broad, and extend to 150 metres in length.

The first thought which struck scholars of prehistory when they began to pay attention to these enormous heaps was that they were shrines. However, the true nature of this early form of environmental pollution did not remain a mystery for long. 'Kitchen Midden Culture' was the name scholars gave to this era. Nowadays the archaeologists speak rather of the Maglemose or the Ertbølle period. Maglemose in south-west Seeland, not far from the Danish village of Mullerup, and Ertebølle in Jutland are the locations of the most important 'Kitchen Midden' sites.

Pits, Traps, and Dangerous Rocks

A bear has the mind of one man and the strength of nine. He is not afraid of a crowd, but he runs away when faced with two brothers for he knows that a man does not love his own life more than that of his brother, whom he never betrays. The Laplanders believe that the bear has a conscience and that he can find no peace in his winter sleep if he has killed a man. Then the Uldas do not look after him and feed him while he sleeps. If the hunter wants to have any luck while hunting a bear he must prepare himself carefully. Dressed in their best clothes the hunters go forth in a definite order and never call the bear by its name. If he is killed, then they try to persuade him that somebody has overcome him because in the next hunt the bear will wreak a terrible vengeance on his conquerors. The dead bear is solemnly thanked for sparing the hunter and a song of joy is sung by the men as they return home. When the women hear the song they adorn themselves with silver and brass ornaments, and suck the bark of the alder tree till their saliva turns red. Using this to paint their faces, they welcome the hunters with a festive song.

The hunters are forbidden to enter their tents by the usual door. They have to lift up the tent flap opposite and enter through that opening. The women take off their caps, spit the chewed alder bark over the hunters and the dogs, and hang brass rings and charms round their necks: the yellow and shining brass is considered to be a magic metal which gives protection against the supernatural power of the bear. Only on the following day when the hunters are rested is the bear brought into the camp and given an equally festive reception. During the meal many rituals are observed. All bones and legs must remain intact. As soon as the meat is eaten a large hole is dug on the spot on which the bear has been killed, and its reconstructed skeleton is laid to rest. Even the tail is not forgotten. The grave is then closed, but it is firmly believed that the bear will rise again and that it will be possible to hunt him once more.

This Swedish folk legend about the Laplanders' bear-hunt describes in detail the last northern European nomads' relationship to the beast of the chase. In their eyes it was omniscient and sacred and anybody who wanted to capture a bear could not simply go out and kill it. That was impossible, or at least very dangerous, because the vanquished beast could avenge itself even after death. It was necessary to placate the creator, the lord of the beasts. The hunter had to conciliate him because he was robbing him of one of his creatures. This was why the Laplanders hunted in their best clothes and went off in full array, and why they were not allowed to call the bear by name. This was the age-old magic of the hunt which protected the hunter from everything evil, because in practising it he honoured the beast.

But it was not enough to meet the creature with respect; that may have made a reconciliation possible and diverted any thought of revenge, but it did not result in a capture. Here, too, powerful magic played its part. An experienced magician must be able to cast a spell over the hunted animal and force it into the pits and enclosures. To this end he draws the animals and portrays their capture with drawings of weapons of the hunt surrounding the scene; alternatively, with his magic power he entices the animal to the place where the hunters are lying in ambush.

Even today before every big expedition the Laplanders and other primitive hunting people make sketches of the animals which they intend to hunt. In 1933 Frederica de Laguna described in the *Journal de la Société des Américanistes* how

30 and 31a, b The Middle Stone Age rock carvings in Norway clearly illustrate the transition from a naturalistic style of art still under the influence of the Old Stone Age (30) to simplified forms (31a) and then to a pronounced stylization (31b).

30 Rock carvings of a stag which was discovered in 1957 near Büla in Norway dates from 5,000 to 4,000 B.C.
31a Rock carving of an animal near Bogge, Norway is the period between 4,000 to 3,000 B.C.
31b The very stylized representation of a stag with internal organs (so-called 'X-ray style') is of approximately the same period.

the Eskimos in south-west Alaska practised this custom. Herbert Kühn also described this ritual as practised by the Pueblo Indians in the Southwestern States of the U.S.A. 'The Indians explained the meaning of the lifeline to me,' wrote the professor. This lifeline has a peculiar significance: it is a custom in the society of many hunting-culture peoples that before the hunt the magician draws not only the outline of the animals to be hunted, but he paints the heart and sometimes other major organs on which mortal wounds can be inflicted with arrows also drawn in the picture. The lifeline which he depicts going from the heart to the mouth is the channel by which life leaves the hunted animal at the moment of death.

This kind of insight into the hunting customs of contemporary primitive peoples helps to clarify the customs of prehistoric time. Three hundred generations back in their migrations to the north, the early Scandinavian hunters carved and scored pictures of this nature onto the walls of the rocks of their native land or coloured them with paints made from iron oxide and fish oil. The oldest of these hunting-culture paintings goes back about 8,000 years, and predates the great period of Ice Age art. These pictures have been engraved onto the rocks with smooth lines and their crude outlines recall the cave drawings from the later Ice Age (ill. 30).

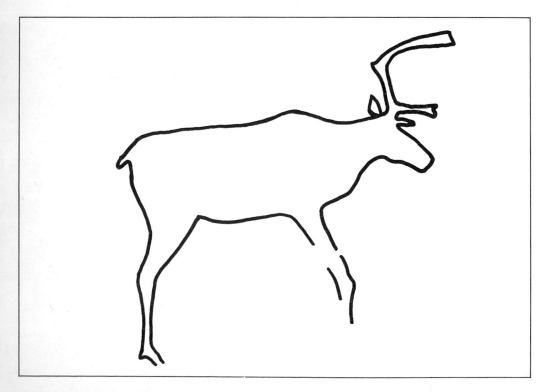

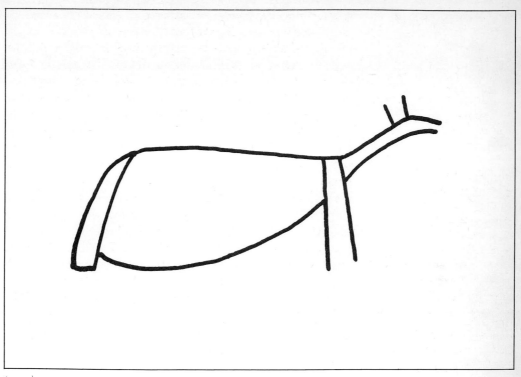

(31a)

(31b)

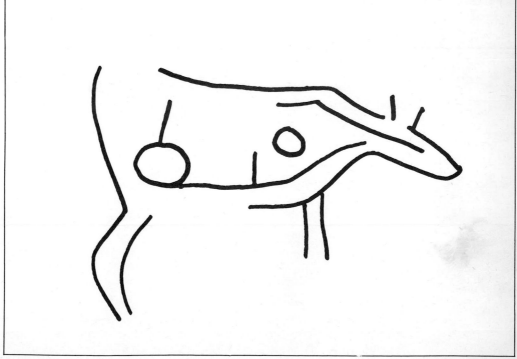

About 5,000 years before our time (3000 B.C.) the animal figures became more rigid, more symbolic and the lines are not merely scored but have been hammered onto the stone (see ill. 31a). The 'lifeline' and some inner organs are also indicated (see ill. 31b). This second period would appear to have lasted for 'only' 1,500 years and in fact only half as long as the first. But most of the Scandinavian rock images originate from this time, which is followed by a third stage of development. This begins to point to yet another period in which naturalistic engravings and paintings give way to abstract drawings and symbols.

With one single exception none of the rock images of the Middle Stone Age in the Nordic countries was executed in caves, which further distinguishes them from the French and Spanish art of the Old Stone Age. But the places where the spellbinding hunting-culture painters engraved and chiselled their life-size, and over life-size, ritualistic hunting pictures are anything but suitable for rock paintings. For example, near Sagelva about 90 kms west of Narvik, high above the bank of the Sagfjord, two huge reindeer are engraved into the vertical sheer wall of a cliff. Anyone who wants to see them has to be let down the side of the precipice on a rope.

Pictures in such an inaccessible place can hardly be mere mural decorations. Their meaning is to be found in ritual. Why did those hunters single out as sites for their spell casting carvings the suicidal cliff walls rising precipitously out of the sea not only around Sagelva, but in many other places in present-day Norway? Again the answer lies in the intent behind the pictures: by means of their magic powers the animals depicted were meant to attract the real-life animals. The hunters drove them in flocks over the deadly crags, and gained an easy prey. This method of hunting was widespread in Norway right up to the end of the last century, and the Laplanders and native peasants continued to practise it in the same places as portrayed in the ancient pictures of Stone Age life. It was only in 1899 that with a new law on hunting the government put an end to this kind of animal harassment.

The Honey Collectors and Waspwaists
As the ice retreated in the Middle Stone Age many wild animals had migrated north and were followed by the hunters. They settled in Scandinavia as far as the North Cape and in Finland and parts of northern Russia. However, not all the descendants of the Ice Age men followed the great 200-year migration. Spain too was populated during the Ice Age, not only in the north in the region of Altamira, but also as far

down as the south coast. This is proved by the fantastic Ice Age paintings found in the cave of La Pileta, in the mountain range of Sierra de Libar 42 kms north-west of the holiday resort, Marbella. The style of these closely resembles those of the late period in Lascaux. But in the same cave there are also paintings which do not fit into the art of the Ice Age. They are abstract drawings, stylized human figures, zigzag lines and hatched squares out of which series of lines emerge as if in bundles (see ill. 32). Scholars of prehistory have discovered that the cave of La Pileta, which is 2 kms long, contains traces of many prehistoric periods, right up to the Neolithic period. The Iberian Peninsula was continuously settled from the time of the Ice Age. While descendants of the people of the Ice Age were conquering the vast land masses of Scandinavia, here everything remained unaltered. The hunt continued on familiar ground and was preceded by the ritual painting

32 The walls of the Cueva de la Pileta, to the west of Ronda in the Spanish province of Malaga, contain a cross-section of paintings covering a period of more than 10,000 years; in this picture the Ice Age paintings are succeeded by the very stylized and already completely abstract sketches dating from the Middle Stone Age.

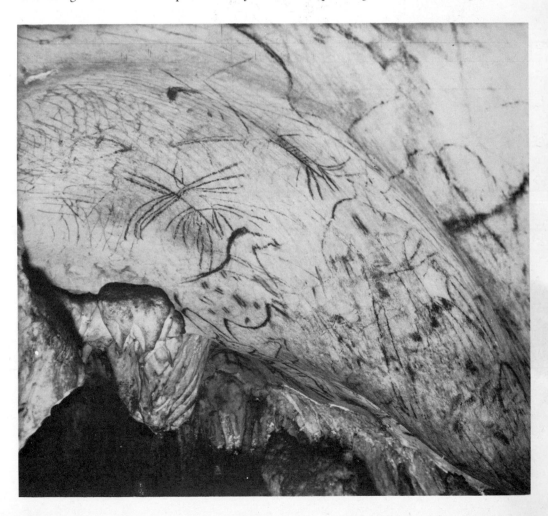

ceremony. But the execution of the pictures changed a great deal. In the late Magdalenian period, the last great phase of Ice Age art, the trend towards simplification had already begun. Representationalism was being replaced by formalism: the naturalistic picture of an animal by the presentation of movement or expression through a drawing of an outline; this style was continued in the Middle Stone Age in Spain and opened the door to completely new methods of presentation.

Following the pattern of Scandinavia nearly all the rock pictures of the Middle Stone Age in Spain are no longer to be found in the inner recesses of the mountains but on vertical or overhanging cliff walls, or even in niches and grottoes.

It was a lucky coincidence that the first important finds of this Spanish Expressionism, which scholars called the rock art of eastern Spain after the area in which it was most widespread, became well known when in Europe there was a similar movement in art away from naturalism to stylization. The French painter Braque, and especially the great Spanish artist Picasso, influenced by Cézanne's work, were conscientiously attempting to limit painting to a surface representation and to free it from such artistic tricks as perspective, or light and shade, and to lead it towards a new and pure form of artistic realism. This called for a new approach to the object seen, an abstraction. The Nordic rock art of the Middle Stone Age had also practised abstraction; it had simplified without disturbing the natural proportions and by this method had come to a kind of formalized presentation of a species. The Nordic magicians did not portray a particular reindeer, but presented the reindeer as a stylized and nameless representative of its species. This kind of abstraction was not the concern of Braque and Picasso. What they were looking for was not the simplification of expression but its intensification. And they soon realized that there was only one way to achieve this. They had to distort the objects portrayed, the landscapes and the figures, to systematically change their shape to accommodate them to a flat surface. Without this stylistic device, robbed of any perspective, the objects would have been lost in a flat and expressionless surface. By this means, however, despite their conscientious two-dimensional approach, the pictures gained a new dimension. As well as giving a purely objective and external presentation it was possible, by means of brushwork and colour, to give expression to the surface of an inner state of mind: excitement, relaxation, haste, patience and detachment. When in 1907 Picasso painted his famous *Demoiselles d'Avignon* he perfected this 'surface expressionism'. He himself said that the discovery in 1906 of Negro

33 In the Valltorta gorge in eastern Spain there are some of the most important finds of rock paintings, a large number of which are to be found on the overhanging parts of the cliffs. This hunting scene is from the 'Cueva de los Caballos'.

sculpture had had an important influence and had reinforced him in his leaning towards stylization.

With this the circle was complete. Negro sculpture of Africa has links with the ancient tradition of expressionism in the rock paintings of the African continent. These are to be found in north Africa in the upper regions of the Atlas and Ahaggar mountains as well as in the extreme south of this vast continent. The African rock carvings and paintings are in turn closely related to the eastern Spanish pictures of the Middle Stone Age. These were the pictures which created such a stir in the first two decades of our century.

In 1906 the Spanish scholar, Juan Cabré Aguiló, reported
on the paintings of Calapatá which he had discovered three
years earlier in a ravine 50 kms north-west of Tortosa. In 1908
a second find with similar pictures was discovered in Cogul,
18 kms to the south of Lérida. In the following ten years there
was a series of discoveries, of which among the most
significant were the rock pictures of Minateda, Morella la
Vella and the Valltorta ravine (see map 3 p. 263).

All these paintings very skilfully depict the everyday life of
the Ice Age. There are huntsmen carefully aiming their bows
and arrows, others charging forward to follow their shot, and
others skilfully ducking as whole herds of elegant red deer are
killed (see ill. 33 and 34). There is the famous scene of the
honey gatherer who has climbed a rope to a wild bee's nest,
with one hand holding a basket and with the other groping
into the honey-bearing opening. The disturbed bees, drawn
as large as pigeons, swarm round him like an onslaught of
giants (see ill. 35). There are pictures of warriors going into
battle, in formation (see ill. 36); fierce battle scenes and
elegant animal figures in full movement, often in the middle of
a jump (see ill. 37). These scenes were always painted in the
flat and never drawn in outline as were those of the same
period in Scandinavia or as those in a third group of less
clearly defined rock paintings in northern Spain (see ill. 38),
which date from the Middle Stone Age. Just as in the early
modern paintings of the 20th century the proportions,
especially of human figures, are distorted. The waists become
long and thin and the arms become spindly lines, whereas hips
and legs are emphasized and sturdy. The gestures of the
warriors in illustration 36 with their exaggerated and extended steps, with the upper part of their bodies leaning far
forward, arms raised in unison, exude an almost supernatural
threat. Even the picture of the leaping capricorn in illustration
37, which at first sight appears to have a naturalistic quality, is
found on closer inspection to be exaggeratedly expressionis-
tic: the elegant flourishing antlers have been greatly enlarged
– they reach almost to the rear of the animal – a device which
underlines the expression of movement. These pictures were
the beginning of a new period in Stone Age art. The ritualistic
concept of thousands of years ago is still there, but the
pictures incorporate other newer features – an element of
narrative and an expression rooted in the innermost being of
the animal which is being painted.

To date scholars have recorded forty finds of these rock
pictures in eastern Spain and many more are expected. (On
map 3 page 263 the more important places are shown.)

34　Paintings of the *Middle Stone Age are rarely as well preserved as much older Ice Age examples found deep inside the caves. Often there is little more than the suggestion of a painting left as is the case on this section of rock in the 'Cueva de la Vieja' near Alpera.*

35　*The painting in red, in the 'Cueva de la Araña', near Bicorp in the Province of Valencia, of bees surrounding a honey-collector, has become famous.*

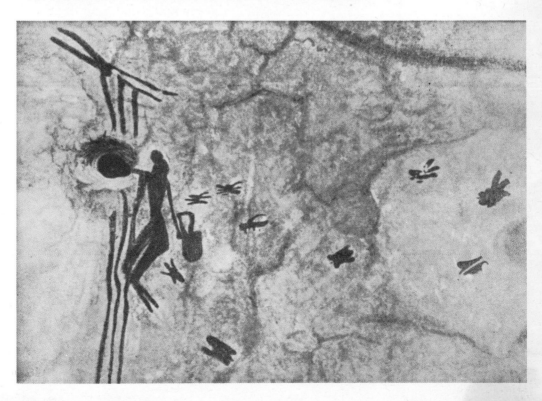

36   The gorge of Gasulla not far from the gorge of Valltorta in eastern Spain (see ill. 33) is one of the most important find places for rock paintings, containing a large number of individual scenes.

37   The eastern Spanish rock paintings (this one is at 'Cueva Remigia' near Ares del Maestre) resemble snapshots with impressions of tension, movement and life.

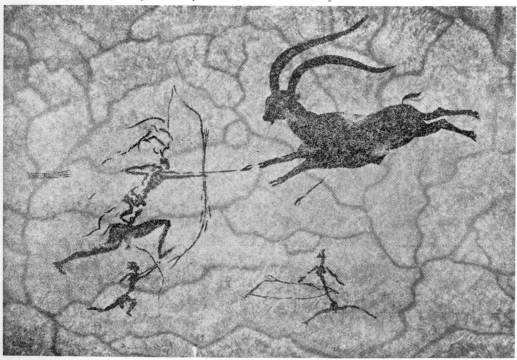

38 In contrast, the northern Spanish contemporary paintings (this one is at Campo Lameiro in Galicia), seem somewhat stiff and lifeless. Nevertheless its simple and stylistically accomplished outlines are very attractive.

The Mysterious Pebbles of Le Mas-d'Azil

Just as Picasso and Braque in their first cubist pictures slowly felt their way from stylization to symbolism and then to comletely abstract painting, the same is true of the eastern Spanish cliff paintings. At another find of the Middle Stone Age (Mesolithicum) the archaeologists came across paintings which clearly anticipated the further development towards abstract art.

The place is called Le Mas-d'Azil and lies on the northern slopes of the Pyrenees, half way between the two small French towns of St. Girons and Pamiers. The landscape of the area is grandiose and exceptional in Europe. The motorist driving along the little river Arize, following Route Nationale 119, coming from the west through a green valley in the middle of delightful chalky hill country, after a sweeping left turn in the road, is suddenly surprised by a huge dark hole in the rocky mountain range which towers in front of him. The river Arize disappears into the huge cave. The motor road, a little further to the right, penetrates the mountains through a tunnel, the opening of which is very modest compared to the entrance to the cave. However, once inside the motorist finds himself let loose in a huge dark enclave. Inside the mountain the tunnel and the cave merge into each other. The subterranean cavern which opens up before him is so huge that it could comfortably house two or three middle-sized cathedrals, one behind the other. It is 30–50 metres wide, some 60 metres high and 470 metres long. It would seem incredible that the little river Arize could have created this mighty tunnel by natural means. But such is the case. It was the work of millions of years. The geological history of Le Mas-d'Azil stretches far back in time. Its significance in human history is also clear. The cave had been inhabited, almost without interruption, for 50,000 years. The first to live here was Neanderthal man, who used it as a shelter from which he went out to hunt the rhinoceros. He was followed in the Old Stone Age by the Cro-magnon man. In the ante-chambers of the great tunnel, which lay deeper in the heart of the mountain he left behind paintings typical of the Magdalenian period. After him Le Mas-d'Azil sheltered the people of the Middle Stone Age and after them the cave was still inhabited for a long time. This is proved by a New Stone Age megalithic structure, a dolmen, not far from the cave. Later the Gauls moved in and built a fortified position on which the Christians later built a chapel. During the Huguenot persecutions 200 defenders of the faith barricaded themselves in Le Mas-d'Azil where they built a chapel. In 1860 the French built the Route Nationale 119 through this natural tunnel, and today there is a car park and a museum of prehistory in the centre of it.

It is clear, then, that Le Mas-d'Azil has always been inhabited, but one period of the Middle Stone Age in particular was, for good reason, named Azilia by archaeol-ogists. As early as the end of the last century, in addition to the stone implements characteristic of the time, strange red pebbles had been discovered in the cave, which were later found to be 10,000 years old. They date, therefore, from the early Middle Stone Age. Since then similar pebbles have been brought to light in excavations in France, northern Spain, northern England and eastern Bavaria.

The pebbles are decorated with circles, crosses, dots, straight and zigzag lines, designs shaped like combs or some

39   Despite some superficial resemblances there is little to support the theory that the peculiar signs on the pebbles dating from the Middle Stone Age found in the cave at Le Mas-d'Azil in western France (upper row) were precursors of lettering forms of the ancient inhabitants of the Canary Islands (lower row), which have been dated as several thousand years later.

kind of plant. With a little imagination, stylized figures of people can be recognized. Ever since their discovery, scholars have puzzled over these pebbles. No satisfactory answer has been found. Some scholars have thrown doubt on their great age, and believe that they may somehow have been influenced by Egyptian amuletic art. Others see them as the precursors of the lettering used in the Canary Islands many thousands of years earlier (see ill. 39). Their real meaning will probably remain a secret for ever.

But whatever the true meaning of these different signs, they marked a decisive step in the movement of art away from representation to symbolism.

THE GREAT AGE OF SYMBOLS

When Ghosts came to Europe

In his *Fanneslied* the anthropologist and native poet from the South Tirol, Karl Staudacher, features the wizard 'Spina de Mul' (the skeleton of the mule) who in prehistoric times, wrought his mischief by night in the region to the west of Cortina d'Ampezzo in the eastern Dolomites. 'Spina was a powerful and dangerous wizard. In his wanderings he liked to take on the shape of a half decomposed mule.' This is how Karl Felix Wolff describes him in his well-known Dolomite stories: 'His head, neck and front legs were covered with skin, but his hind quarters were nothing more than a skeleton. Spina trotted on his front legs and dragged his skeleton behind him. From time to time he let out a savage cry. Nobody wanted to meet him, as he wandered by night through the woods and wilds, because he was immune to gunshot. If anyone tried to attack him with a spear or a knife he knocked the weapon out of their hand with a magic spell, snarling and baring his enormous mule's teeth until his opponent took flight.'

Spina de Mul owned the miraculous 'Rayéta', the luminous stone which was known to be of priceless value. This stone later came into the possession of the King of the Fànes, a mighty mythical kingdom set high up in the mountains where today lies the desolate rocky wilderness of the Fànes Alps. How the King of the Fànes acquired the Rayéta is no longer clear. There are several different versions in local folklore. One thing is certain, that the king gave the jewel to his charming daughter and that she wore it in a tiara to the end of her days. After her death the mule skeleton cast a spell under the influence of which a raven stole the precious stone and dropped it into a deep mountain lake, where it was watched over day in and day out by a fire-breathing dragon. In these mountains there lived dwarfs who collected treasures. They worked their way underground towards the precious stone, but each time that they came close to it the dragon picked up the Rayéta in its claws and flew off with it to another mountain lake. As it flew through the night skies it left a fiery trail in the sky.

This ghost-bird was familiar not only to the folklore of the Dolomites; in the Vintschgau there is also the same legend of the dragon-like creature which flew through the night with a precious stone in his claws.

When was this time about which the old legends tell? Did it really exist? It would appear so. When Wolff was travelling around in the south Tirol collecting his Dolomite legends an old Ladin*-speaking native from Enneberg had assured him

* A Rheto-Romanic dialect.

that the tales from the Fànes were much older. Again, another man from the Gader valley had explained to him that a castle had once stood opposite the gap of St. Cassiano in the mountains, that a king had waged war there, and that later everything had gone to ruin.

In 1953, many years after Wolff had written his stories, the archaeologist and engineer from Bolzano, Georg Innerebner, found the remains of an old civilization high up in the stony wildernesses of the Fànes Alps. Describing the prehistoric fortress situated at a height of 2,600 metres he wrote:

'Out of the sinister heap of ruins there emerges, like the tracks of an underground train, a semi-circular stone wall, some 50 metres long, several metres high and 4 metres wide at the top. It is easy to imagine the part hidden under the stone rubble which completed the circle measuring 60 metres in diameter and 200 metres in circumference, and covering an area of 3,000 square metres. In the centre there would appear to have been a construction which had collapsed in a heap. Cursory digging on the crest of the mountain, in the pass and on the summit of the Burgstall uncovered typical examples of burned earth and fragments of roughly hewn objects to which it is difficult to give a date due to the lack of characteristic markings. It can however be assumed that they belong to the late bronze or early Hallstatt period (about 1200 to 1100 B.C.).'

The summit of the mountain near this ruin of the fortress is still called the 'Burgstall' which is the old name for a fortified place.

The legendary Fànes kingdom did in fact really exist (see ill. 40). But what is the truth about the spitting mule skeleton and the fire-breathing dragon? Did they exist? Certainly not in reality, but very definitely in the beliefs of the peoples who inhabited the Alps 3,000 years ago. So did the dwarfs, elves, hobgoblins, gnomes, ghosts of the air and wood goblins, the supernatural and subterranean creatures which still live in our old fairy tales – they all date from this era. In those days they were part of daily life. Men lived with them asking the good spirits to protect them and exorcising the evil ones. At the same time they painted and engraved them in thousands and tens of thousands onto the rocks of their homeland, not only in the Dolomites but over the whole of Europe. They are still to be found everywhere: from the west coast of Portugal to the Black Sea, from the storm-swept north of Scotland and the Norwegian fjords to the islands in the Mediterranean. They appear on stone, sometimes ravaged by time, on surfaces of

glacier, on rocky promontories, and on the perpendicular walls of caves. They can be found by romantic mountain streams, in wild gorges and on the high Alpine peaks where the marmot is found. They inhabit rocky cliffs lashed by wind and sea, and dusky caves. Over 300 finds with pictures of ghosts and gods and other abstract figures have already been discovered in Europe. In some of them there is only one lone picture while in many there are dozens, and in others there are tens of thousands.

From where did the ghost-like creatures come? They did not yet exist in the Middle Stone Age. Witchcraft and magic were certainly there and also the belief in one great god, the master of all beasts. But ghosts were unknown in the Middle Stone Age. Nowadays scholars believe that ghosts and goblins actually 'immigrated' into Europe and that they came from the East, from Asia Minor and Mesopotamia. The belief in ghosts was common in those parts, and it spread with the trade that was beginning to flourish throughout the Mediterranean area. It spread to Troy, Cyprus and the Greek islands as well as to Crete, then to Sicily and northern Africa, and at last also to southern Spain. It fell on especially fruitful soil in this region, as it is especially rich in rock paintings depicting mystical figures (see ill. 41). From Spain the belief in ghosts spread slowly further afield until it penetrated the whole of

40 Prehistoric mountain peoples have left strange traces in many parts of the upper regions of the Dolomites. On the 2,174 metre high summit of the Puflatsch near Castelruth (Castelrotto) is the throne-like 'Witches' Seat', cut out of the augitporphyry rock, with majestic views into the Grödner and Eisack valleys.

41   During the 5,000 years before Christ European rock paintings were very stylized and sometimes even completely abstract as these symbolic figures near Fuencaliente (province of Ciudad Real) in Spain show. These paintings are 4,000 to 6,000 years old.

Europe. This, of course, did not happen overnight – it took several hundred years, but it had come to stay. In all later phases of prehistoric art, from the New Stone Age (Neolithicum) throughout the Bronze Age to the Iron Age, the ghost is always present. It has remained part of the popular belief even into our times. Many remote rural areas of Europe are still haunted by ghosts.

With the appearance of ghost pictures, rock carvings and paintings turned more and more towards the Abstract. By the Middle Stone Age period the tendency towards stylized painting had grown. Painting and engraving moved away from simple representation and inclined towards symbolism. This development reached its peak around 2000 B.C. There are many rock paintings which remind us of the abstract designs of the Spanish painter Miró. Symbols dominated every picture. Different symbols were used in different regions for men and women, for animals, water, rain, dwelling places, fields, sun and moon and many other things (see ill. 42a, b, and 43a, b).

In northern Europe where the hunters were also cattle-breeders, abstract forms of supermen appeared on the rocks, representing the ghosts of ancestors out of which male deities gradually developed: Wotan the victorious, Odin with the lance, the mighty Thor or Donar swinging his hammer (see ill. 44).

Man	Ghosts	Animals	Ox and Plough
Fuencaliente Ciudad Réal Spain	El Ratón Guadiana Spain	Carschenna Graubünden Switzerland	Fontanalba Mont Bego France
Barranco de la Cueva Aldeaquemada Spain	Vallée des Merveilles Mont Bego France	Bohuslän, Tanum Vitlyke Sweden	Naquane Valcamonica Italy
Tomba Branca Sardinia	Los Gavillanas Ciudad Réal Spain	Cemme Valcamonica Italy	Bagnolo Valcamonica Italy
Foppe di Nodro Valccamonica Italy	Tarascon-sur-Ariège France	Naquane 47 Valcamonica Italy	Bohuslän Tanum Tegneby Asperget Sweden
Gran Faetto Val Chisone Italy	Cueva de la Graja Jimena, Jaen Spain	Vallée des Merveilles Mont Bego France	
Vallée des Merveilles Mont Bego France	Grotta Scritta Olmete Corsica	Lonbo da Costa Ponte Vedra Portugal	**Rock art symbols of the Early stone age Bronze age and Ice Age**
Ardegais Maia del Porte Portugal	Luine roccia 57 Valcamonica Italy	Uffington Wiltshire England	
Bohuslän, Tanum Vitlycke Sweden			

42a In the whole of Europe the New Stone, Bronze and Iron Ages were for a time strong in mystical symbolism and belief in ghosts. This table shows a selection from the large number of more or less abstract signs of that period.

42b In Savona in June 1974 a collection was shown of abstract paintings dating from thousands of years before Christ. From left to right: Fentans (province of Galicia, Spain), Carschenna (Grisons, Switzerland), the Valley of Pinerola (Piedmont, Italy), Mont Bego (Alpes Maritimes, France), Tanum (Bohuslän, Sweden).

43a and b   The meaning of the abstract signs on the Petra Frisgiada, a large boulder in the North of Corsica near the menhir shown in illustration 2, still remains unexplained.

The agricultural peoples of middle – and especially southern – Europe, on the other hand, worshipped female deities. The earth which receives the seed in the spring and bears fruit in the summer is the link. Our idea of 'Mother Earth' has the same origin. Even at the present time the cult of the Madonna and the worship of the Mother of God are most strongly rooted in the countries of southern Europe. In the rock paintings of prehistoric times the divine mother figure, the *dea Madre*, the great mother, the *Magna Mater* appears constantly, especially in Italy (see ill. 45 and 46). The goddesses of the south, Isis and Demeter, go back to this period and many old customs of the Alpine countries such as the nocturnal wooing of the beloved one, recall the esteem in which woman was held in the past thousands of years. Many Alpine legends tell of old mountain peoples ruled by women who were much honoured as great leaders. There was Tanna, the queen of the Crodères who, with her face hidden by a veil and a blue crown on her head, sat in the dusky ice palace of Cornón de Fròpa in the innermost recesses of the Marmolada mountain range; Dona Dindia near Cortina d'Ampezzo, the gentil-donna della Fratta who lived in the mountains near Rocca Piètore, and the Fànes Princess Dolasilla who was immune to all magic spells.

44 The Nordic collection of legends, the Edda, describes the great Germanic god Thor as having a wheel with four spokes as a body, the head of a goat and wielding a powerful hammer in his right hand. The Swedish rock paintings at the site of Tegneby near Tanum in the district of Bohuslän represent him in exactly the same way.

45 (opposite) Under the symbol of the sun at the upper end of this stone column from Bagnolo in the Valcamonica there is an abstract sign: two series of concentric circles and above them a collection of horseshoe-shaped lines. Archaeologists interpret this as a symbol for the great Mother Goddess, the Magna Mater, who was held in high honour by the agricultural peoples of the central and southern parts of Europe.

46 Stylized pictures of the Magna Mater, are to be found as far as the interior of present-day Denmark. The zigzag lines on this piece of pottery are a symbol for water which brings fertility to the fields.

The linguistic origins of the term 'Fànes empire' are uncertain. One explanation has been put forward by the German scholar, E.H. Meyer. He talks of 'Venetians or Fenes people' and goes on to say: 'The empire of the Fenes people becomes in time Venice or Venusberg.' The expert on these legends, Wolff, comments: 'This link with the idea of Venusberg seems to me especially important because Venusberg is a matriarchal kingdom with a woman at its head.' From the cultural point of view the Europe of the New Stone, Bronze and Iron Ages is very much of a unity, in fact a 'United Europe' of prehistoric times, in spite of all the different races and in spite of all the changes over the centuries and thousands of years. The same spiritual outlook, the belief in ghosts which dominated everyday life, the cult of the ancestors, the worship of many gods instead of one God – all united the peoples from south to north, from west to east. The many similar rock paintings and engravings in the most varied parts of the continent are evidence of this all-pervading spiritual unity (see ill. 41 and 42).

The pace of development varies according to time and geographical regions. In the warm, carefree countries of the South new cultural influences spread faster; in the countries of the North more time is needed to break the links with the past. In the remote valleys of the Alps myths and old customs live longer than in the large trading communities along the Mediterranean coast. Bronze and later iron came into general use in different parts of Europe at different times. History is fluid. It is impossible to make sharp distinctions either in time, place or in respect of spiritual development. Beliefs and customs overlap in time and space to produce a new religion, or they continue to exist side by side with external differences but inspired by a common spirit.

The strict division of the last four thousand years B.C. into the Early Stone, Bronze, and Iron Ages, which is the theme of so many history text-books, has probably done more harm than good to the understanding of the peoples of this period. No serious scholar of the history of civilization would have been so misguided as to think that men of the 20th century would have changed fundamentally in their outlook as they learned to use new artificial materials. Why then should the men of the New Stone Age have become different human beings as they learned to use bronze and later to work iron as a new material?

It would be better to lay more emphasis on the common elements in the spiritual and intellectual life of that period instead of making the customary division of the period into three; the New Stone, Bronze and Iron Ages, the dividing lines between which can hardly be identified except through objects found in the course of excavations. They certainly cannot be distinguished in time, because, for example, bronze came into use in the eastern Mediterranean region more than a thousand years earlier than in central Europe, and in Russia it took several hundred years longer. Nor can they be distinguished in space because various peoples, especially in the Alpine regions, used bronze objects long before they learned to work this metal or to mine it. It was first brought to them through commercial exchanges. And the same applies to iron.

The concepts of the Bronze and Iron Ages may be very meaningful to the archaeologist who is following local excavations, or to the scholar who wants to draw conclusions about early trade routes and racial connections from the different periods in which the metal came into general use in

Europe. But these concepts are of little help to anybody who wants to take a wider view of things, for whom man himself, his intellectual environment and his emotional and spiritual life are the things that really matter.

During the last 4,000 years B.C. there were, of course, spiritual differences between the various peoples in the great civilizations of Europe, and as a result also differences of expression. But these differences cannot be attributed to the use of bronze or iron ore. They grew according to districts, conditioned by the natural surroundings in which a people lived, by the climate and living habits. There were many differences of outlook within the framework of the unifying philosophy of that period. Many well-preserved finds bear witness to this.

Sources of Writings in the Mountains of the Gods

Like an artery the Route Nationale 204 winds across the country from Nice towards the north-east into the peaks of the Alpes Maritimes. It takes the traveller through picturesque valleys and rocky gorges, over five mountain passes with superb views, to the Italian frontier. 13 kms before reaching the last pass, the Col de Tende, the top of which crosses the frontier, lies the small mountain village of St. Dalmas. From there a small asphalted road climbs up to the west through a wild and romantic alpine valley to La Minière-de-Vallaure. This consists of a group of houses with an electricity power station on the edge of a romantically situated artificial mountain lake. Anyone who loves the mountains and does not shrink from walking at great heights is in his element here. A range of mountains nearly 3,000 metres high offers a variety of magnificent climbs on all sides, pleasant strolls along the mountain ridges, or fell walks on a series of peaks with magnificent views. The stony track or narrow cliff path leads the nature lover on what is hardly a mountain climb past nearly half-a-dozen dark or bright green alpine lakes, several of which remain frozen well into the month of June.

At the parking place under the power station of La Minière there is a signpost pointing the way to the Vallée des Merveilles, the Valley of Wonders. In the heat of the midsummer sun of the southern Alps this 3,000 metre climb up to the mountain valley can be something of a strain. In early summer, however, up to the middle of June, when thousands of white anemones are in full bloom in the light green woods of cembra pine, when the mountain meadows on the first part of the climb are filled with bright yellow primroses, and when at the higher levels the fresh cool streams of the melting snows flow over the fields, the traveller will find his rucksack easy to carry and his heart will be filled with the joy of living.

It is indeed a world of wonders up there in the mountains round the Vallée des Merveilles. But the wonders to which the name refers are of a different kind. They are wonders of the world of the fantastic which surround an Olympus-like seat of the gods.

Other names in the higher regions near the Valley of Wonders indicate this: 'Le lac du Diable' (devil's lake), 'Valmasque' (Valley of the Magicians), 'Vallée de l'Inferno' (Hell Valley) or 'Cime du Trem' (Trembling Mount). In the middle of these mythological places, there stands supreme the lofty peak of Mont Bego, the Mountain of the Gods nearly 3,000 metres high (see ill. 47). The root of the Indo-European word 'Beg' denotes the divine lord and master. The title of the Ismaelites' divine princess 'Begum' contains this syllable.

Two mountain valleys near Mont Bego are especially worthy of a visit, the Vallée des Merveilles and Fontanalba. There in the middle of the orange-coloured and green-tinted mountains the visitor will find the explanation for the origins of the names of the lakes, mountains, and valleys which would seem to belong to a fairy-tale: 40,000 pictures carefully chiselled into the smooth surface of the stone. It requires some practice to be able to interpret these symbols. Time has long since given them the same orange-green colouring as that of the surrounding rocks. Anybody who has begun to understand the meaning of these symbols will find it hard to leave these desolate heights. He will find everywhere new pictures, symbols of weapons and people, mysterious rectangles with dots and subdividing lines inside them, repetitions of geometrical shapes, squares with horns, ovals and triangles. These are the signs of cattle, symbols of fertility for the cattle-breeder who thousands of years ago chiselled them here with stone implements and metal stencils (see ill. 48, 49 and 50). The existence of these pictures, which are situated at a height of 2,000 to 3,000 metres, and which for 9 months of the year are buried under ice and snow, has been known for a long time. There are records of them which date back to 1650. But it was only 200 years later that the French scholar Emile Rivière discovered their prehistoric origin. After him, a number of scholars made systematic studies and catalogues were compiled. The most important of these men was the English botanist, Clarence Bicknell, who in the course of 39 years found and copied 12,000 separate pictures; the Italian

47　Mont Bego towers 3,000 metres above the Valley of Wonders (in the foreground) where the larger rocks are covered with carvings.

48　Among the most frequent subjects depicted in the carvings found in the valleys round Mont Bego are weapons such as this halberd in the shape of a scythe . . .

scholar Bernardini and recently Robert Hirigoyen whose archive today contains some 40,000 drawings. There is not much variation in the themes of the engravings which were dedicated to their Master by our ancestors, the Ligurian tribes living round the seat of the gods in the southern Alps. This is to be expected as symbols do not leave much scope for variety. Today our traffic signals, which are after all nothing but symbols, are also not easily changed. They are the same everywhere, and it is this fact which makes them symbols.

Generally speaking, the signs on Mont Bego can be divided into six groups. Into symbols for cattle (see ill. 50), symbols for weapons (ill. 48), symbols for people (ill. 49), agricultural symbols, which represent oxen ploughing (ill. 51), symbols for fields and grazing land and lastly geometrical signs which are not easy to understand. The frequency with which these different signs are found varies a great deal. Cattle and

49   . . . human figures are seldom portrayed . . .

50   . . . symbols of cattle are frequently . . .

weapons have the first place. Symbols representing people only make up 0.5 per cent; of these, half are linked with drawings of ploughs which are relatively frequent. Of particular interest are three painted figures which are very

51 . . . sometimes two stylized oxen, yoked together and pulling a simple hooked plough (see also ill. 42a).

different from all the others. These are 'the magician', 'the Magus with the face of Christ', 'the tribal chieftain'. The scholars Bicknell and Bernardini believe that these pictures did not originally look as they to today. They hold the view that they developed out of the old typical symbols for cattle and weapons by the addition at a later date, though still in the prehistoric era, of lines joining them together (see ill. 52). It is probable that these figures did not represent magicians and chieftains as they are generally called, but that they were pictures of gods or the souls of ancestors. The 'hands which point upwards' with outspread fingers on the head of the magician would seem to support this interpretation because the Egyptian Ra (the soul) was traditionally represented with raised arms and open hands.

There is no doubt that there was a link with the old civilizations of the East. This is of particular interest in connection with the development of the alphabet. Our A, for example, goes back to the old Phoenician lettering, as does the first letter of the Arabic alphabet, the alif, and the Greek capital letter *Alpha* (A). This on the other hand was very close to the cattle symbol of Mont Bego and *aliph* in old Phoenician and in Hebrew does in fact also mean *oxen*. The symbols for oxen on the holy mountain in the Alpes Maritimes were nothing other than the precursors of an alphabet in pictures.

A similar situation exists with our letter B. It also can be traced back to Mont Bego. There the sign for a house was a rectangle with a dividing line drawn inside it which divided it into two rooms. Our B and the Greek capital letter B look very much alike even today. But *Beth* in old Phoenician and in Hebrew means an open nomadic tent, the *house*. The word appears again in the biblical town of *Bethel*. In *Genesis*, chapter 28 Jacob says: 'This is none other but the house of God' and two verses later we read how Jacob gave the house the name of *Beth-El. El* is the Hebrew definite article which follows the noun. It is not by chance that the letters A and B are the first letters of our alphabet, and that the alphabet itself is named after these two letters, as it was in the past, in which it has its origins. A stood for cattle and B stood for the house, the two basic things around which all else revolved. They were the symbols for the maintenance of life and home.

The mountain wanderer who walks up the high valleys round Mont Bego is at the same time climbing to the very sources of our letter-based script, the foundation of all western civilization.

52   Prominent students of the rock carvings found around Mont Bego believe that the few pictures of gods and ghosts were not created all at once, but originate from retouching of existing carvings representing cattle. The illustration shows on the left a completed figure, and on the right the possible stages in its completion.

Camuni – Rocks Reveal the History of a People

In 1931 the Italian scholar Paolo Graziosi, a Florentine publisher of technical magazines on anthropology and ethnology, reported on two boulders with prehistoric carvings which had just been discovered near the small village of Cemmo near Capo di Ponte 35 kms north of Lake Iseo (see ill. 53 and 54). Graziosi had discovered 275 separate carvings of deer, cattle, goats, other animals and daggers on the two sandstone boulders.

In the following years and decades the scholars of rock carvings made many other finds of prehistoric stone engravings in the neighbourhood of Capo di Ponte. By 1970 600 locations with more than 2,500 separate pictures were known. It was about the same time that the Italian Professor Emmanuel Anati with the help of students and natives of the Valcamonica, was carrying out his systematic and intensive investigation, which had begun 14 years previously, of the thickly wooded cliffs at a height of over 1,000 metres, in the valley of the small river Oglio. In 1975 the tireless scholar wrote in the introduction to a new text-book on prehistoric art in the valley, 'By far the most important and richest collection of rock carvings in Europe at the present time is that of the Valcamonica, where over a stretch of 70 kms in a narrow

53 In 1909 Dr. Laeng discovered in front of the small village of Cemmo near Capo di Ponte in the Valcamonica two large lumps of rock with prehistoric carvings, the 'Massi di Cemmo'. One portrays mostly deer and a series of indefinable animals, and daggers . . .

Alpine valley more than 130,000 prehistoric figures have been discovered and where there are without any doubt still an unknown number of pictures waiting to be discovered.' (see ill. 53 to 57).

No less than 20 books and more than a hundred articles in scientific journals were published between 1960 and 1975 on the rock carvings in the Valcamonica, and nearly all of them were well illustrated. When this attractive scholar remarked with a smile that till now less than five per cent of all the prehistoric carvings in the valley have been catalogued, he testified to the enormous number of rock carvings in the immediate and more distant neighbourhood of Capo di Ponte.

In the year 16 B.C. Roman legions occupied the Valcamonica and incorporated the valley into their mighty empire. The people they subjected are described in their

54 . . . the other one is decorated with the gentle forms of human beings, animals and daggers, probably dating from an older period . . .

55 (opposite) similar dagger forms are the main subject in a rock covered with carvings which now stands in the garden of the study centre of Professor Anati in Cemmo. As in many other rocks of this kind, the whole series of carvings is dominated by a symbol of the sun. Professor Anati considers this to be a mark of an old cult of the Sun.

56   Again and again the visitor to the Valcamonica will come across symbols of human beings, simple 'stick figures' of little men with clumsy bodies and raised arms . . .

writings and in their triumphal arches in the same way as the Ligurians of Mont Bego. They call the valley Camuna and the inhabitants Camuni. It was a small community with its own 5,000-year-old history which lost its independence with the Roman conquest.

'From then on the existence of the pre-Roman Camuni remained unknown for 2,000 years,' says Professor Anati. 'And it might have remained so for ever,' he continues, 'if the Camuni had not left such a legacy of historic and artistic beauty, unrivalled by any other prehistoric people after them.' Professor Anati is referring to the rock carvings. Based on them he has carried out a twenty-year work of detection and a step-by-step deciphering of the history of the people of Camuna, their morals and their customs, their social organization, their contacts with other peoples, just as if he had been quoting from an open history book.

Some six or seven thousand years ago the Camuni came to this very inhospitable Alpine valley in search of new lands. They were probably fleeing before the agricultural peoples who were pressing down in large numbers into the fertile plains of the river Po. In the first period the Camuni lived nearly exclusively from hunting and cattle-breeding as the soil of the desolate valley could only be cultivated with the

57 . . . or rectangular figures like this one from near the Hoario Terme. This kind of simple representation of the human form goes back as far as six or seven thousand years.

greatest difficulty. The earth was marshy, the mountain slopes were covered with hundreds of torrential streams and bespattered with moraine and boulders.

Some three thousand years before Christ the Camuni acquired new neighbours, the Remedelliani, who probably came from eastern Europe and settled around Brescia. From them the Camuni learnt how to handle new weapons and implements. From them they also learnt how to work metal and to till the fields.

About 2000 B.C. the Camuni adopted from their neighbours the halberd, a weapon which by then had come into use all over Europe. They also took over from them the hooked plough, one of the most important discoveries of the Stone Age. They carefully reproduced in thousands of rock paintings every new object in general use.

The Camuni soon established neighbourly relations with other peoples as well as with the Remedelliani. They also gradually exchanged practical experiences with other civilizations (e.g. the Aunjetitz and Polada).

Around 1600 B.C. there was a major change. The Mycenaeans established a powerful commercial empire in the Mediterranean area, which reached the Valcamonica. They exchanged arms and other commodities for the metals which were common in the Alps and amber from the north. This was in great demand and came down as far as the Adriatic sea along the old amber trade route which went along the river Elbe, the Saale or the Moldau and the Inn, passing by the Valcamonica. The contact with the merchants from Mycenae left a deep imprint on the Camuni. They adopted Mycenaean arms, especially the dagger, and learned about the wheeled chariot and many other inventions.

Trade with the Mycenaeans lasted for 200 years. After that, relations were severed and the Camuni established new links with other peoples. For those who could read the language of the 'Pitoti', which was the common name given to the rock pictures, there were clear indications of the influences of the great central European cemetery urn culture, the 'Padane' or pile-dwelling culture (see ill. 58), and later the most important

58 At about 1,000 B.C. the ancient inhabitants of the Valcamonica carved into the rocks images of huts which were mostly forms of pile construction. The figures on the lower right-hand side of the picture appear to portray a sexual act.

of them all, the Hallstatt culture. The representations of the sun, for example, which appear again and again on the rocks of the Valcamonica and the neighbouring Valtellino are the same as those which decorate the pottery of the period of the pile dwellers.

A far stronger influence than that of the Mycenaeans on the Camuni was that of the Etruscans around the turn of the 7th to the 6th century B.C. Always susceptible to new influences they soon adopted the customs and habits of the Etruscans which were prevalent in central Italy at that time. They copied their weapons, dressed as they did and learned from them the art of lettering (ill. 59). They began to chisel the new letters into the rocks of the valley, using Etruscan lettering to make words of their own dialect, which was similar to the Rhaetian language. This brings them to the

59   The Camuni, the ancient inhabitants of the Valcamonica, began to learn the art of lettering from the Etruscans some time about 1,000 B.C. The letters of the alphabet were often written from right to left as in the case here with the word 'ENOTINAZ', found on a rock near Campanne di Cimbergo. On the extreme left can be seen a typical Rhaetian 'Z'.

turning point from prehistory to history, the period of which written evidence exists. This transition occurred with sudden violence throughout Europe. In addition to the Etruscans the Illyrians in the south, the Celts in the north, the Gauls and Iberians in the west spread out over Europe. The various cultures intermingled and traditions of the Camuni which had lasted for thousands of years grew weaker and weaker. The Celtic influence, with the famous La Tène culture, was the last foreign force to be felt, and from then on the ancient little mountain tribe began to lose its identity and become a mere appendage to the Roman Empire. A 'modern' world had overtaken Valcamonica and its inhabitants abandoned their ancient custom, which had lasted for 150 generations, of chiselling pictures of everyday life into the rocks of their native land.

The military occupation under the Emperor Augustus signified the formal incorporation of the Camuni into the Roman Empire in whose cultural orbit they had already been for a long time.

With this fusion of cultures the memory of 500 years of history had become so faint that until 1931 nothing was known about the ancient mountain people except its name. Even that was to be found only on the Roman lists of subjugated tribes. But then the scholars discovered the rock carvings of the Valcamonica and these began to release those secrets which had been hidden under an ever increasing blanket of moss and mould for over two thousand years.

Maps of Stone

Among the most common and at the same time puzzling pieces of evidence of prehistoric times made of stone are the cup forms. These are round cup-shaped hollows, a few centimetres in diameter, on the surfaces of cliffs. The largest of these measure some 10 to 15 centimetres. They are to be found in all the countries of Europe, in the whole of Africa, America, Russia and even in Australia. They appear in the plains as well as in the mountains, in the interior as well as on the coast (see ill. 60).

The people of the Old Stone Age cut them into the rock and so did tribes of the Middle and New Stone Ages. They were traditionally believed to be at least 30,000 years old when the scholar Denis Peyrony, the expert on the Ice Age, who with Abbé Breuil was one of the champions of the authenticity of the Franco-Spanish cave paintings, made a sensational find in his excavations on 17th September 1909. Under the over-

60 (opposite) The 'Stein des Wilden' (Pierre des Sauvages) above St. Luc, not far from the path to the Bella Tola in the Val d'Anniviers, is one of the most beautiful cup form carved rocks in the Alps. The entire surface is covered with deep bowls. In order to photograph them effectively the cup forms in the foreground were filled with water from a nearby sacred spring.

hanging cliff of La Ferrassie he discovered a stone slab with 18 cup forms cut out of the rock in prehistoric times. It was possible to fix a date for the stone slabs by the examination of the layers of earth and the skeletons of two adults and two children. It was 100,000 years old! It had not been created in the Old Stone Age by Cro-Magnon man, but by someone from a much older and already extinct race. The cup form was the work of Neanderthal man! The practice of making these mysterious little hollows was therefore 100,000 years old and continued apparently without any serious interruption into the period of the Early Stone Age.

Many a volume has been written about these little cup forms. How much speculation have they raised and how many different interpretations have been built into them? In the beginning many scholars thought that these cup forms were not the work of man but the result of some climatic forces or even the work of some animal or other. These scholars could not have seen the most important of these stone cup forms, otherwise they would have recognized at first sight the deliberate shaping of the little moulds and the obvious use of tools in their creation. Near the cup forms are often found incisions in the shape of crosses or circles.

Nowadays many scholars believe that stone cup forms were built in shrines to honour the dead. In these, offerings in the form of food and drink were put out for our ancestors, or oil lamps were burned in their honour. Instead of the ancestors, fertility gods could equally well have been honoured in this way. Prehistoric man was anxious to win favour through the gifts that he placed in the little cup forms. The rocks into which these were cut would then have been sacrificial altars. There is much to support this interpretation. On the other hand, against this theory is the fact that many of these rocks had a very sloping surface. On these the little hollows would not have been able to hold any solid or liquid gift. The sacrificial offerings would therefore have either fallen or run out of them. Another argument against the theory of an altar was that many of these rocks were unsuited by their position to be used as community sacrificial centres. On the steep surround it would not have been possible for more than two or three of the faithful to assemble.

Cesare Giulio Borgna, architect, town-planner and enthusiastic student of rock carvings, developed a new theory working with the centre for the study of prehistoric art in Pinerolo. In his office, which is decorated with copies of stone carvings, he explains to the visitor: 'Naturally our interpretation does not fit all of these rocks, because they made their appearance independently in many different parts of the world and at very different times in prehistory. But we think that we have discovered the true significance of the rocks in the mountains and high valleys around Pinerolo. These rocks are always found in exposed places and command a panoramic view of the valley. Does this not indicate that the bowl or cross shaped signs in these lofty places point to something that lies in the valley below?' Cesare Borgna has been following up this thought quite objectively and with scientific thoroughness. There are in this region many rocks with carvings dating from the Middle Stone Age: symbolic human forms, suns, stars and all kinds of puzzling geometrical signs and of course again and again cup forms (see ill. 61 and 62).

First of all there is the lump of rock of Prato del Colle (which means 'Meadow on the Hill') on the top of a mountain, 1,730 metres high above the little village of Gran Faetto on the northern slope of the Chisone valley. A spring rises immediately next to the rock. Similar springs are found near many of the rocks which have cup forms cut into them. Is there therefore some connection between the water and the little cup forms? And if the carvings also point to something in the valley, do they indicate places where water can be found?

61   The valley west of Pinerolo is an Alpine centre of abstract rock carvings. This rock surface on a mountain slope, not far from the little village of Gran Faetto high above the Chisone valley, contains a number of deep, engraved crosses, which are symbols of human beings (compare ill. 42a).

62   An important stone carved with cup forms is the Rocio Clapier, a rock which stands alone on a mountain slope overlooking the little community of Sappè in the alpine pastureland of Pramollo (compare 'RC' on the map in ill. 63b).

63a (opposite, above) The Italian expert on rock carvings, C. Borgna, believes the Rocio Clapier is an old stone map. Crosses stand for human settlements or places of temporary shelter; deep cup forms stand for springs and circles for common pastureland. The numerous little shallow cup forms near the deep hollow marked 1 signify high growing vegetation; the

This seemed a bold conjecture, but Borgna followed it up. The cup forms made in the rock of Prato del Colle are connected with one another by deep fluted furrows. If the cup forms are really symbols for places where water is found the furrows must represent water ducts. The older inhabitants of the little mountain village nearby remembered stories of the existence of a small artificial stream which once took the water flowing down from the Gran Clot and was said to supply some of the highest of the mountain huts and also the village of Gran Faetto which did not have springs.

Borgna devised a plan which he then put into execution. As he said, 'Water always flows downhill, that is why an aqueduct must first have passed by the settlements situated higher up the mountain, then by those lower down and so on. If you examine the contours of a good physical map it should be easily possible to reconstruct the course of an artificial stream of this kind.' On Borgna's enlarged map two different ducts could be detected. Their course coincided exactly with the flutings in the rocks into which the cup forms had been cut.

Was this a coincidence? Armed with a map and a compass a student carefully followed the lines drawn on the map on the ground. Sure enough he found traces of ancient irrigation systems and below them, well worn projections of rock which

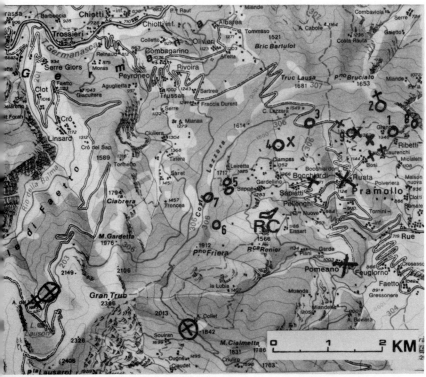

dotted lines mark the boundary of the mountain pastureland of Pramollo. (The above picture of the large surface of the rock has been put together from seven separate photographs and is quite accurate.)

63b   Marked on the map of the district around Pramollo are many of the places where traces of water and human habitations have been located which Borgna had discovered on the stone map of Rocio Clapier.

clearly revealed the existence of a prehistoric track running alongside the duct.

Borgna concluded that rather than being mystical symbols of a religious cult, the cup forms were signs which had a real-life significance. Another piece of evidence from the Stone Age supported his theory. The 'Rocio Clapier' is a prominent rock 1,190 metres high from which there is a view stretching over the valley of Pramollo (see ill. 62). On to its surface of 12 square metres, in addition to a great number of large and small cup forms, our ancestors had carved crosses and circles. In the New Stone Age the cross was a very simplified symbol for human beings. Was it intended to indicate on this 'map' the presence of human beings in settlements or at least places of temporary shelter? In fact, Borgna found near the remains of prehistoric dwellings in the area a few signs of crosses scored onto the rock which supported this hypothesis. On the stone walls of enclosures, which were presumably prehistoric animal cages, he and his colleagues discovered circular signs. Do the circles on this stone 'map' signify fences?

Borgna took exact measurements of the 'Rocio Clapier' and also accurate photographs of the rock from a height of 4 metres. The results seemed to confirm his guesses. Most of the larger cup forms corresponded to springs in the ground, while many crosses corresponded to remains of ancient settlements or to mountain hamlets which still exist today (see ill. 63a and b). However, in spite of a great deal of evidence, Borgna's 'map' theory is still only a working hypothesis. But it should be followed up by scientists because there is more in favour of this than of other attempts at an interpretation of the cup-forms. Many of these other attempts are well on the way to being accepted because of their constant repetition in technical journals and books. Since the summer of 1975 Borgna and the study group of Pinerolo have been trying, in the excavations which they are conducting around Pramollo, to find additional material to support or refute their theory.

What Scholars Do Not Talk About
The Valcamonica, Mont Bego and the valleys of Pinerolo are certainly great names in the history of rock carvings in the Alps, but they are by no means the only ones. The mountains of Italy, Switzerland and Austria are littered with traces of prehistoric times.

In the Swiss canton of Wallis there are examples of cup forms, amongst the most beautiful of which are the 'Pierre des sauvages', immediately above the small village of St.-Luc in the Val d'Anniviers, and in the 'Heidenplatte', above the village of Zmutt at the foot of the Matterhorn (see ill. 60).

Another beautiful rock with cup forms is the 'Hexenstein' which it is possible to reach in about an hour by following a well-marked track which runs from Terenten in the Puster valley along the Winnebach valley up to the log cabin in the woods.

Like the rocks with the cup forms in the valleys round Pinerolo, the rocks of 'Pierre des sauvages' and the 'Hexenstein' are also situated close to springs. Our ancestors considered a fresh mountain spring to be a sacred place to which they brought offerings certainly connected with a fertility rite. Between the Achensee and Steinberg in the Austrian Tyrol there is an ancient holy spring which rises in a mountain meadow lying between the rocks near the footpath leading from the Guffert hut to the summit of the Guffert mountains. In 1957 Rhaetian inscriptions discovered near this spring and dating from the time around the Birth of Christ were deciphered. One of them says: 'Here is water'. The others refer directly to sacrificial rites:

'To Kastor Frau Etuni made her offerings here.'
'Frau Ritali made her offerings to Kastor here.'
'Here Frau Mnesi made her offerings to Kastor.'
'Usipe, the prisoner, made offerings here.'
'Here Elvas fetched water.'
'The votive picture was offered by Estas.'

To the ancient tribes who tilled the land water stood for fertility, and it is very probable that the cup forms near springs had some kind of meaning in the fertility rite. This does not necessarily contradict their significance as 'stone maps' in accordance with Borgna's theory. If these 'maps' indicated places where water could be found in the valley, and if these were sacred for our ancestors, then the maps were certainly also sacred.

But the English scholar Rivett-Carnac, who lived in India, had towards the end of the 19th century already given a different interpretation to the stone cup forms. He too saw a connection with the fertility rite. According to Rivett-Carnac the making of holes in the rock signifies nothing more or less than a symbolic mating with Mother Earth. He bases this theory on customs which are still practised in India today. A similar view is taken by Friedrich Schnack, the poet and author of travel books on Madagascar. He tells of natives who during hot tropical nights literally 'love' the earth, flinging themselves on it and passionately embracing it as though it were a beloved woman.

For the ancient tribes of the Alps many of the large, holy

stones were steeped in fertility magic. In Castelfeder in the
Italian Tyrol not far from the little village of Auer (Ora in
Italian) there is a slide made of stone, a smooth polished block
of rock, where, ever since the Bronze Age virgin girls wanting
to find a husband or have a child would slide down on their
bare bottoms. Similar slides are common in the whole Alpine
region and this fertility rite was continued to a certain extent
in some places till the beginning of this century. Similar rites
were practised right up to the present in the extreme north-
west part of France, in the ancient land of Brittany, which has
always had its own, separate culture. There young girls who
longed to get married would go stark naked into the moonlight
to rub their navels against 'hot stones', and childless couples
would go out at night to make love by these pagan shrines.

On the 'Hexenstein' the witches stone near Terenten, mentioned above, which was most certainly also a fertility rock,
our Bronze Age ancestors did not carve just cup forms into the
rock. It is also possible to distinguish quite clearly the imprint
of a human foot chiselled into the stone. In places this symbol
on the rock carvings is relatively frequent. Sometimes it is
found on the huge stone tables of the Valcamonica (see ill. 58).
A particularly beautiful example of a rock with many foot
imprints lay for many years in a meadow in front of the
romantic old Swiss mountain village of Soglio im Bergell,
west of the Maloja pass. In a literal sense this stone has had a
very *mouvementé* past! How it was found is described by
Giovanoli, an authority on local history:

'On 10th September 1922 a goatherd came to me beaming
with joy to report that, high up on the mountain, in the middle
of the Bügna pine forest, he had seen a rock with clearly visible
footprints on its surface. I immediately went to the spot and
found in the pine forest on the mountain slopes which shut off
the valley to the west of Soglio at a height of 1,600 metres an
unevenly formed lump of rock lying on top of another one. On
its uncovered surface next to some circular cup forms it was
possible to see small, faint imprints resembling human feet.
To all appearances the rock had rolled down from a height.'

Later this remarkable prehistoric find was brought down
the mountain by the local authorities and set up as a tourist
attraction in the meadow outside the village of Soglio. It has
now reached the last stage of its journey and stands in the
Swiss Federal Museum at Chur.

Various scholars of prehistory have given many different
interpretations to the foot imprints on the various ritual stones
in the Alps, in Scandinavia and to the sites with rock carvings
in the Sahara. The well-known authority on rock carvings,

Professor H. Kühn, sees them as symbols indicating the presence of the gods, whereas the author Karl Lukan in his book *Excursions into the Alps of Prehistoric Times*, maintains: 'Surely one pictures the gods as large and powerful and not as having dainty, ladylike feet. Furthermore: why so many footprints on one stone? Hence another interpretation: the footprints are those of brides and were chiselled into the stone at the marriage ceremony. They were in fact marriage documents made of stone.' Unfortunately Lukan does not say how he came to this conclusion or from where he had adopted it. But there are more than physical clues to support this interpretation.

When I was wandering off the beaten track through the southern parts of Tunisia, I found myself on the way to Guermessa, an out-of-the-way mountain oasis west of Foum Tatahouine. People of the half-nomad Ghoum tribes live there in cave dwellings which have small walled courtyards in front of them. The oasis stretches along a grandiose and desolate mountain desert at half the height of the two neighbouring peaks. This is all that is left of an ancient tableland. One of these peaks has already been worn down to a smooth round dome and out of the reddish-brown no-man's-land of the desert the other sticks up like a chimney (see ill. 64). Accompanied by a young native and walking on a track covered with camel dung which was as springy as turf, I

64   Members of the semi nomadic tribe of the Ghoum live in cave dwellings in the mountain oasis of Guermessa, situation in a rocky desert area deep in southern Tunisia. The dwellings go right up to the foot of the vertical walls of rock which support the summit. This mass of rock situated above the highest, now uninhabited, caves is an ancient sanctuary

65   *This picture shows some of the dozens of footprints engraved in the stone next to prehistoric*
cup forms. The footprints are of newly married couples and to this day are chiselled into the rock.

penetrated the upper parts of the village. It was like walking along a road into the past. Some of the higher rock dwellings were abandoned, those uppermost had fallen into decay and could well have been five or six centuries old. An easy climb took us over the last lap of the ascent up the massive rock. At the top we were surprised to find rock carvings. On the stony plateau we first noticed dozens of chiselled footprints, some of very ancient and some of very recent origin (see ill. 65). I then noticed cup forms which must undoubtedly have dated back to prehistoric times. This was proved by the patina which covered the carvings. The rock on which we were now standing was an ancient sanctuary. All the figures next to the foot imprints, some of which were in Arabic and others in European script, referred to very recent dates: 1940, 64, 66, 14.4.66, etc. Next to them in Arabic script were the Christian and surnames. I asked my companion the meaning of all this. 'It is an ancient custom,' he replied in broken French. 'This is a holy rock. When a couple get married people come here from all the oases and celebrate in Guermessa for three days and three nights. Then they climb this rock and chisel the footprints into the stone as well as their name and the date. They continue the celebrations in Guermessa for a week and then they go home again to their oasis.' I asked how old was this custom. 'It has always existed,' was the prompt reply.

Just as the North African rock carvings are linked with the rock paintings, especially in Spain, to a common origin, so the Tunisian custom of engraving the imprint of a foot very likely has its origins in the same ancient rite as that which was practised in the Alpine regions.

In both areas these rites were often preserved for centuries, which was a thorn in the flesh of the Christian Church, particularly in the Middle Ages. The Church endeavoured, often unsuccessfully, to wean its lambs from the worship of Pagan deities. Then the Church resorted to a cunning device. They decided to combat ancient magic with newly invented magic using the sign of the cross to banish witches and evil spirits. Such a sign of the cross is clearly visible, chiselled into the slope of Castelfeder as well as on some of the rocks with carvings on Mont Bego and in the Valcamonica. In distant Russia the Christian Church also used this method to exorcise images of the Middle Stone Age gods which were found on the shores of Lake Onega. Furthermore, near the 'Pierre des sauvages' in Val d'Anniviers a weatherbeaten old wooden cross can still be seen today.

Many other places with rock carvings in the Alps were brought within the Christian orbit by prelates of the Middle

Ages by means of crosses and holy inscriptions.

The scholars excavated a whole series of new carvings only a few years ago. But most of them do not talk about it for a variety of reasons. Many of the serious scholars of prehistory are still rankled by the reproaches which were directed against many of their colleagues in the past three-quarters of a century because of errors in dates, or premature reports on insufficiently established finds and sometimes even for forgeries. Nowadays scientists want to be certain before they give publicity to their new discoveries. Accurate and unambiguous dates cannot yet be given to the majority of the most recent finds. That they go back as far as prehistoric times is also not one hundred per cent proved, although two famous scholars, Professor Kühn and Ernst Burgstaller, are very nearly convinced of it.

The second reason for the reticence of the scholars is explained very eloquently by Herbert Nowak, the Secretary of the Institutum Canarium, an Austrian society for the study of prehistory, in one of its annual reports. 'During the past twelve years the chief centres of our excavations were the Tennengau region and the area around Lofer in the province of Salzburg, but part of the work was conducted also in the region of the Rupertiwinkel in Bavaria and in the Salzkammergut in Upper Austria. In two places in neighbouring Upper Austria near the gorge of Kienbach, not far from Bad Ischl and in the 'Höll' in the hills of the 'Toten Gebirge' (Dead Mountain range), visitors could see the devastation caused by the exaggerated publicity given to these places. Well-meaning reports in the mass media generally bring thousands of sightseers who photograph, draw and sometimes even perpetuate themselves by scrawling on the rocks which contain carvings from the past. For this reason it is preferable not to mention any places by name to avoid the danger of destruction. That is also the reason why the excavation of the rock carvings in the Bluntau valley was conducted for many years with the requisite precautions. Work was carried out only in autumn because in spring and in the summer the valley was visited by huge armies of tourists whose attention was purposely not drawn to the rock carvings, for the reasons mentioned above. It is still not possible to say with certainty what damage the publicity given to the engravings at St. Wilhelm in the district of Taugl has done to them. In any event, for their protection, newspapers are not supposed to give any names of the places where rock carvings are to be found.

'In the past few years we discovered the following rock

carvings. We took the necessary precautions for their protection and preservation.' Then Nowak lists twenty-two finds of
rock carvings in Tennengau and Pinzgau, all made between
the years 1960 and 1971, and he concludes with the words,
'We know of many more places, but they have not yet been
fully explored.' (See ill. 66.)

66   *Ancient signs for houses and other artists' symbols near Wegscheid,
Dürrnberg in Austria.*

For these reasons, this book deliberately does not contain
any accurate description of the places where finds have been
made which are insufficiently authenticated or which cannot
immediately be recognized. Anybody who is really interested
in ancient rock carvings will certainly find his way to them,
and will get further assistance from a school teacher,
clergyman, or mayor with good local knowledge. The
appendix to this book contains a list of technical publications
which can be consulted; in addition, the Institutum Canarium
at Hallein in Austria, which has already been referred to, will
prove to be a useful source of information.

Two more relatively well-known sites of finds should be
mentioned since they have already been given publicity in
various media. They are the rock engravings on the
Tschötscher heath (see ill. 68) which can be found in the
vicinity of the large S-shaped curve in the little road between

Brixen and the mountain village of Tils (about 1.5 kms from Brixen), and the important rock carvings in the Toten Gebirge (see ill. 67). They are situated in the 'Höll', a rather sinister and very romantic piece of country lying at the foot of the rocks which form the summit of the Stubwies. These are easily reached from the Linzer Haus to which a cable-car runs from the Pyhrnpass road. The guardian at the hut will gladly explain the site of the rock carvings which are a little more than a quarter of an hour's walk away.

67 (opposite) The Tschötscher heath near Brixen in the South Tyrol is one of the lesser known find places of prehistoric times. The 'Mule-Symbol', the meaning of which is still not clear, is frequently found here.

68 A rock carving out of the 'Höll' in the 'Toten Gebirge', Austria.

Strange Circles

Were the rocks with the cup forms sacrificial altars? Borgna, the expert on rock carvings from Pinerolo, and many other eminent scholars contest this, and their scepticism is thoroughly justified by the fact that many of the cup forms in the Alpine region are to be found on more or less sloping rock surfaces. How much more credible, on the other hand, is the 'map' theory! Although there is so far no concrete proof, the existing evidence hardly leaves any more room for doubt. According to this theory, rocks with cup forms were definitely not altars. Whoever adopts this line of argument should not concern himself with prehistory, otherwise he could be in for a shock. W.B. Morris, the Scottish expert on rock carvings, was told by a farmer's widow on the island of Seil in the Firth of Lorne in Scotland that in her youth, some 50 years ago, the inhabitants of the island used to fill the hollow of a cup form with milk once every spring. That was an offering for the 'wee folk', for the fairies. The people believed that if the fairies did not receive this milk, a spell would be cast over the cows. As a result the cows would then give no milk during the whole summer.

Morris told the ferryman of Kerrera, another island in the Firth of Lorne, about this pagan custom which had survived for so long on the island of Seil. The old man then recalled that the farmer from Point-of-Sleat farm on his native island of Skye had practised the same custom when he was a young man. Morris was also told by an inhabitant that on Islay, the southernmost island of the Inner Hebrides, the old custom of making an offering of milk had been generally followed until quite recently. And on the nearby Scottish mainland in the district of Knapdale in Argyllshire, next to the old chapel of Cone there is a cup form which was also used by the farmers to make their offerings of milk right up to the beginning of this century.

Were the cup forms after all places where offerings were made? This may have been true for many of them, but certainly not for all. It seems that in many instances the act of making the cup forms was more important than the cup forms themselves. The natives of the island of Islay from time to time still make the age-old stone hollows deeper and hope that as a result their wishes will be fulfilled. This ceremony appears to go back to a pre-Christian rite. Morris, who was familiar with Scottish customs, considers that it might have had something to do with sun worship. But the cup forms may have been used for much more mundane purposes. On the west coast of Argyllshire and on the island of Tiree experts such as the late L.M.Mann found and made a record of many large hollows which had been carefully cut into very hard gneissic rock. The cup forms were always very close to the water level, not more than a metre above or below it. Morris was able to throw light on the mystery of these cup forms. Two old fishermen from different parts of the island of Tiree told him that in their youth they had used the hollows in the rocks. They were stone mortars in which they had ground mussels, snails, bits of crab and other small sea-food which they used as bait for catching fish. They enticed their quarry into fish traps made of two rows of large stones placed in the shallow tidal waters. The stone mortars for the bait even have ancient Gaelic names: 'Croichtican' or 'Crotagan'. They are always to be found near the richest fishing waters.

Anyone who is looking for a common meaning which will fit all cup forms is wasting his time. Although here and there the hollows in the rock reveal their local secrets, the recarving of them, which recurs again and again, poses an almost insoluble riddle. In the southern Scottish counties alone there are, according to the records of the scholars of prehistory, 50 find sites with circles. In many cases there are a number of concentric rings with a definite cup form as their central point. In most cases the circles appear in smaller or larger groups, and often with single cup forms (see ill. 69 to 72).

69   The cup forms with concentric circles are some of the most puzzling rock carvings. They are particularly frequent in Scotland, such as this find of Drumtroddan near Port William in Wigtownshire, . . .

70   *Many of the cup carvings at Drumstroddan are combined with circular designs,*

71   *as well as those at the important site Achnabreck, north-east of Lochgilphead in County Argyll,*

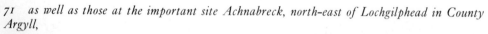

Sometimes there are grooves which extend outwards from the hollow in the middle of the circles. On occasion they lead well beyond the largest of the concentric circles, or join one group of circles with another. Sometimes the outermost circles are not completely closed. Then the whole group looks superficially like a spiral. Now and then there are examples of actual spirals (see ill. 73). It is, of course, not only in Scotland and on the Scottish islands that these circles are to be found. They occur further south in England (see ill. 74), and Ireland is a veritable mine of cup forms and circles (see map 4 on page 264).

72   and near Kilbride House, two miles from Kilmartin (Argyllshire) and in dozens of other places.

73   Single or double
spirals are also occasionally
found in Scotland. This
rock carving is at
Hawthornden some 10 miles
west of Edinburgh.

74   This is the 'Panorama
stone' on Ilkley Moor in
Yorkshire.

There has been no lack of attempts at an explanation of these mysterious symbols. But so far none of them has been completely satisfactory. Everything is pure speculation, and attempts to fathom the puzzle range from serious scientific working hypotheses to fantasies run wild.

Towards the middle of the last century one of the first to discover circles in Ireland, the Reverend Charles Graves, interpreted them as being the ground plans or maps of neighbouring fortifications dating from the Ice Age. He could not have known that the incisions in the rock were two thousand years older than the nearby forts.

Likewise in 1850 the English parson, William Greenwell, saw the circles which he had found in the county of Northumberland as maps of the nearby tumulus graves, according to which a cup form represented a single burial and each ring round the cup form stood for an additional burial in the same grave.

By 1865 in England, George Tate recognized that the whole matter was not quite so simple:

'I cannot see them (the rings) as the pastime of idle soldiers nor as the ground plans for camps, or the practice exercises of budding engineers, because their widespread distribution and their similarity, despite differences in detail, prove that they had a common origin, and point to something symbolic which gave expression to a popular idea.'

Tate's words went to the root of the problem. How can it be explained that such extraordinarily similar symbols decorate rocks in regions which are so far from each other, and what could be their common spiritual origin? What do these signs really mean? Tate was not able to find the answers to these questions. Mysteries have always encouraged guesswork and this is especially true in the case of mysteries connected with prehistory. Most of the 'explanations' of the circles turn out to be ingeniously elaborate attempts at a solution of an unusual mystery, rather than well-founded scientific theories. According to some of the wildest speculations the strange circles were nests of vipers, melting-pots for metals, the remains of knife sharpeners, mortars, early letterings or symbols made by masons, oil lamps, anvils, or failing any of these simply the work of the Druids, those Celtic priests of pagan times who in England are thought to be responsible for so many things that cannot be explained. The Druids have to answer for everything.

Other serious-minded attempts at interpretation involve oracles or altar stones on which blood or other liquid offerings were made. Some years ago Professor Stuart Piggott and his colleagues made much of a possible connection between find places with circles, and deposits of copper and gold. At that time the professor explained the circles as magic signs made by prehistoric men in search of metals. Ronald W.B. Morris, who made an intensive study of the cup forms and circles in the south of Scotland, and also followed up the theory of Professor Piggott, found that in fact some 84 per cent of the engraved stones were located near deposits of copper or gold. However, this high percentage falls to only 65 per cent in many regions in Scotland, and in some districts with well-preserved examples of cup forms and circles, such as the south of Scotland and the south of Ireland, there are no deposits at all of gold or copper.

An attempt at a completely different kind of explanation goes back to Nathan Heywood, who, in the last century, had already written about the circles and 'ladders' on the Panorama Stone of Ilkley (see ill. 74): 'The ladders may have been intended as symbols for some kind of mysterious link between the earth and heaven, or the planets . . . the cup forms and the rings represent planets and the added (outer) circles were intended to give to the planets the appearance of movement. I venture to put forward the suggestion that the images were used as diagrams by astrologers or by star- or planet-worshippers.'

That was indeed a bold theory, but it was certainly not the only attempt at an interpretation based on astronomy. Other authors saw in the circles heavenly bodies revolving round a 'supreme central force', or charts of the constellations Hercules, Corona Borealis, the Little and Great Bear. If it was absolutely impossible to find any convergence with the real constellations, the scholars who were making these imaginative interpretations suggested that they might be the reverse side of astronomical charts, from which the magicians of prehistoric times could take copies on skins for their own use.

Amongst those who had studied the cup forms and rings, the scholars in favour of an interpretation relating to the stars received encouragement from Professor Alexander Thom. He had found cup forms on or near stone structures which were closely connected with astronomy. More will be said about these structures later.

Another interpretation could be possible: in prehistoric religious images different signs for water were very wide-spread all over the world; waves, zigzag lines, stylized rain-clouds, symbolic pictures of waterfowl, etc. Water was essential for life, water brought fertility, the magicians and the ancients prayed to the gods for water. How is water depicted in a drawing? What does water look like? The lines which represent water and are so familiar to us are themselves very abstract in form. In nature they do not occur in precisely the same form. It is, as it were, a cross-section of an agitated surface of water. Groups of concentric circles are immediately recognizable in water when, for example, the first drops of rain fall in a pond or when a stone is thrown into it. It is easy, therefore, to represent water by a series of concentric circles. The central cup form, for example, would then represent the cause of the ripples, the plunging stone. In favour of this theory is the fact that concentric circles appear independently of each other in many prehistoric cultures all over the world. The precedent existing in nature would provide the common origin for all the different representations separated in space.

The Abbé Breuil also played a part in the great guessing game of providing a solution to the mystery of the circles on the prehistoric rocks. He had a great advantage over his predecessors: when he was once in Dublin showing the eminent archaeologist Professor R.A.S. Macalister some photographs of Spanish mural paintings of the New Stone Age, the latter immediately thought of prehistoric engravings in his native land. He later wrote about this event: 'I suddenly remembered the magnificent print of the rock of Clonfinlough ... I took the volume out of my bookcase and laid it next to the photographs. My visitor immediately confirmed that the Irish rock and the Spanish paintings resembled each other both in style and in intent, and that there was undoubtedly a connection between them.'

The two scholars of prehistory concluded from this that Spanish immigrants had brought the Irish circles into the country, and Breuil saw in the abstract Irish images symbolic translations of the Spanish Mother Goddess – in putting forward this theory his enthusiasm undoubtedly led him too far.

Nevertheless it is indisputable that there is some link between the Spanish and the Portuguese rock images and the cup forms and circles found in the British Isles. The pattern of figures found at Lombo da Costa near Pontevedra in Spain and the rock carvings at Fentans in the province of Galicia in Spain so closely resemble those found in Britain that they could easily be mistaken for each other (see ill. 75a, b and c). But does this really mean that traders or settlers from the Iberian peninsula brought these symbols to the islands lying between the Atlantic ocean and the North Sea? Eoin MacWhite who, around 1946 was one of the first to study intensively the rock images in northern Portugal, was firmly

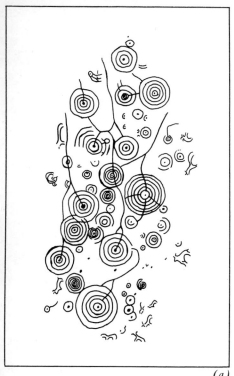

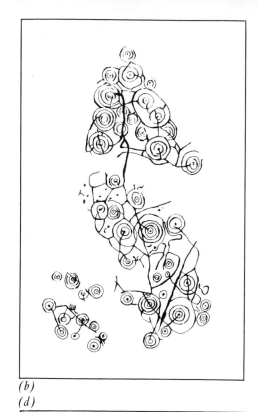

(a)   (b)

(c)   (d)

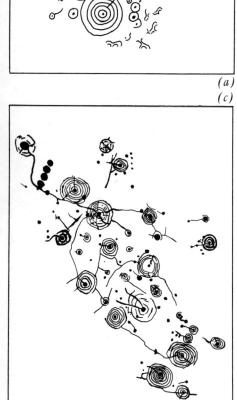

convinced that this was so and international professional opinion came to the same conclusion.

But modern techniques for determining the age of objects resulted in the case being re-opened within a very short time. Many Irish cup forms and circles very probably date from the Bronze Age, although there is reasonable certainty that some go back as far as 3,000 years B.C. They are therefore presumably much older than comparable Spanish and Portuguese engravings, all of which appear to have their origins in the Bronze Age. When the dates coincide, the circles are more likely to have come to Spain from Britain than the converse. They are therefore not the legacy of Spanish immigrants into Ireland, but evidence of a maritime trade which went from Ireland to the Atlantic coast of Spain. There are some excavation finds which indicate this and give support to this theory.

The international reputation of prehistory scholars was again in the clear until 1965. In that year the Swiss forestry expert Peter Brosi was looking, under the moss and humus, for a suitable point from which to take measurements of the pastureland of Carschenna, not far from the parish of Sils in the middle of the canton of Grisons. By chance, in the course of his searches he discovered, on ten large rock tables on the northern side of the crest of a mountain, numerous prehistoric engravings: actual cup forms and circles (see ill. 75d and 76,

75 (opposite) Concentric circle carvings have been discovered in Portugal, Spain, and Switzerland which resemble each other amazingly (a) Lombo da Costa in Portugal, (b) Fentans in Spain, (c) Achnabreck in Scotland (see ill. 71), (d) Carschenna in Switzerland.

76 Until 1965 the rock carvings on the mountain of Carschenna in Switzerland were hidden beneath a thick cover of moss and humus. Now archaeologists are testing them to find out what causes more damage: the sun and wind, snow and rain, or the acids of a humus covering. According to the results of the tests, it will be decided whether the carvings will be kept covered or uncovered. The illustration shows rock table II.

77   On the outer gently sloping shoulder of rock table II there is a group of nine concentric circles, the largest group found so far in Carschenna.

78   Altogether ten rock tables with carvings have been discovered in Carschenna. This illustration is of table III, with its outer cup forms (above left) concentric circle forms and a wheel with spokes, perhaps a symbol for the sun.

77 and 78). Their marked similarity to the rock images in the British Isles cannot be a matter of chance. No less than 13 out of the 16 different basic motifs established in the rock carvings near Derrynablaha not far from Kenmare in Ireland occur also on Carschenna. Which of these versions is the older one? We do not know. How did the patterns reach the Alps from the British Isles? Did they reach the mountains by a detour through Spain? Or do the true roots of this rock art lie on Carschenna? We do not know – it is true that scholars everywhere are making efforts to find answers to these questions, but it still appears as if the many secrets concerning the circles will never be resolved.

The triangle of north and west Spain, the British Isles, and central Switzerland, contains the greatest number of mysteries because of the great similarity of the motifs to be found in it. However, cup forms and circles are also to be seen elsewhere. Near Castelfeder in the South Tyrol Pietro Leonardi took photographs of cup forms and concentric circles which may be related to those of Carschenna. Similar representations are to be found in the Valcamonica (see ill. 79). It is easy to understand that these too could have had a connection with images found in the British Isles, for amongst

79   The archaeologists also found rocks with concentric circles in the Valcamonica, such as this block which comes from near Ossimo and measures 1.1 metres by 1.2 metres.

the Valcamonica images there is another theme which is also to be found in England: the Swastika (see ill. 80a and b). And then finally there is still the secret of the labyrinths, strange figures which at first seem to resemble the symbols of the cup forms and the circles, but are constructed quite differently.

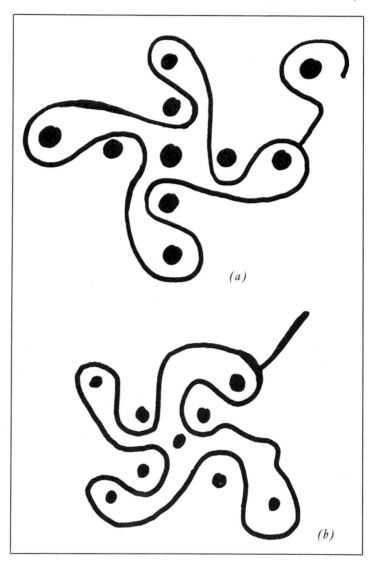

80a and b   The Sistrum was an old Celtic musical instrument. It had the shape of a swastika. Scholars found it reproduced on a number of carving covered rocks in several European countries such as Spain, England, Scandinavia, and Italy. The figure (a) is a swastika from Addingham-Highmoor near Ilkley in Yorkshire; the figure (b) is a rock carving from Giàdighe near Capo di Ponte in the Valcamonica.

Three such labyrinths are known to exist in the British Isles, the Hollywood Stone, which is now in the national museum in Dublin, and two rock carvings in Cornwall near Tintagel. They appear to be of very recent origin and perhaps to date from early Christian times. But the symbol itself is older. It is to be found in nearly the same form in the Valcamonica and in Galicia (see ill. 81a to d).

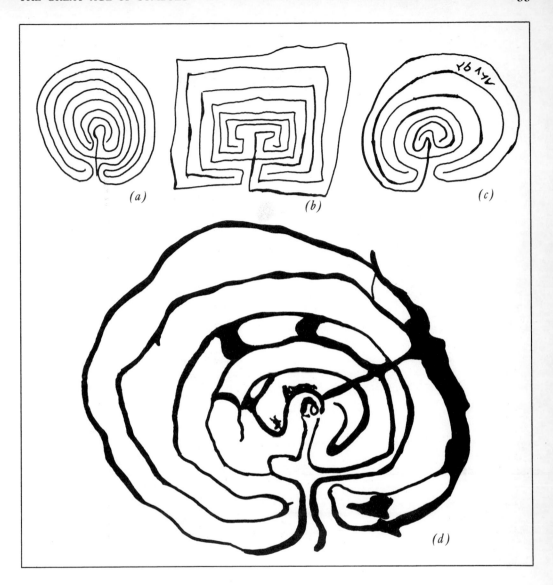

(a)

(b)

(c)

(d)

A linguistic study of the roots of the word labyrinth leads through the Greek back to the old Cretan-Minoan culture in whose domain the most famous of all labyrinths was to be found. On the orders of the King of Minos Daedalus was said to have constructed it for the legendary Minotaur. According to the legend the hero Theseus was the first man who found his way out of its confusing paths, and that only with the help of Ariadne's famous thread.

By following the trail to Crete and to Knossos, the capital of the Cretan-Minoan empire, the scholars were able to throw considerable light not only on the word labyrinth, but also on the design of the labyrinths which were carved into rocks in

81a to d   The labyrinth design was widespread throughout Europe from the earliest of times. Figure (a) is from a carving in the Rock Valley near Tintagel, England; (b) of a sgraffito painting in Pompeii; (c) is from a representation of a knights' tournament on an Etruscan vase; (d) is a rock carving in the Valcamonica.

Europe. In the 3rd century B.C. Knossos issued stamped coins among which there was one with exactly the same image as appears on the labyrinth in Ireland. The question immediately comes to mind, does the Minoan labyrinth go back to the ancient Irish symbol or is the converse true? The answer is equally immediate: we do not know. It was from Crete that the labyrinth gained its worldwide reputation, but there are indications on the old Irish rocks that this symbol might have developed out of the much older cup forms and circles. Later in historical times the figure of the labyrinth gained in importance and spread further and further over the whole of Europe. It is to be found on Etruscan vases where it appears together with figures of riders to illustrate the story of Troy about which Virgil wrote; it is also found in a graffito painting on a wall in Pompeii, as a mosaic on the floors of the houses of wealthy Romans, and embroidered on the robes of the emperor. It became one of the important early Christian symbols and well into the Middle Ages decorated walls and floors of churches, among others the famous 13th century cathedrals of Chartres, Amiens and Reims. In England the designs of labyrinths were cut into lawns, and even Shakespeare in his *Midsummer Night's Dream* refers to the custom of holding games in these labyrinths. The Christian Church gave an allegoric meaning to the labyrinth. The design represents life, open and inviting at the beginning, entangled on its journey and secure in the calm of the spiritual peace reached at the end, which is the central point of the labyrinth. Perhaps this symbolic interpretation as well as the design itself go back to the times of the first labyrinths or even of the mysterious circles and cup forms which are surrounded by legends.

White Horses and White Giants

Ride a cock horse to Banbury Cross,
See a fine lady upon a white horse.
Rings on her fingers and bells on her toes,
She shall have music wherever she goes.

Perhaps this simple English nursery rhyme about the fine lady on a white horse has a very old history. The legend tells of Lady Godiva who once rode through the town of Coventry on a white horse with nothing to cover her body except her long tresses of hair which reached down to her hips. In Finchampstead in the county of Berkshire and in other romantic places in this spirit-ridden island ghostly white horses appear on dark nights to all too credulous ghost-watchers. They trot restlessly through the darkness and disappear just as mysteriously as they appear.

It certainly requires a great deal of luck to come across one of these ancient legendary creatures whose history goes back thousands of years. In all that time the animals must have become just as weary as the time-honoured customs revolving on these revered white four-legged beasts which survived well into the last century.

Anyone who does not believe in ghosts but would like to see one of those mysterious white horses should follow the railway line from London to Bristol. He will find what he is looking for 17 kilometres outside the town of Swindon, near Uffington in the Vale of the White Horse. On the upper slopes of a long table-shaped hill: a ghostly white horse of huge dimensions. With its brilliant white colour the animal stands out sharply against the vivid green of the English grass. It measures 112 metres from its head to the tip of its tail (see ill. 82).

This ground carving is not immediately comparable with others in Europe – and not only because of its size. It is in fact neither a painting nor a rock carving. Its shape is regularly cut

82 The White Horse of Uffington near Swindon near the London–Bristol railway line is 112 metres long and one of the largest rock images in the world.

out of the ground. The thin covering of green grass is removed so that the chalky stone of the subsoil defines the outline of the unusual beast.

No-one knows for certain how old the White Horse of Uffington is. In any case it would have been overgrown with vegetation, if it had not been spared this fate by the ancient custom which has been maintained for many hundreds of years. Every seventh year on Midsummer Night it is 'restored' by the local population. They hold a Midsummer Night festival on the top of the hill above the White Horse, and in the course of their games they carefully remove the overgrown grass and the weeds from its shape. Another custom was linked with this rural festival which is unusual but not confined exclusively to England. The farmers used to roll cheeses down the slope under the White Horse, perhaps as the relic of a fertility ceremony, perhaps as a later version of the pagan fire wheels which the sun worshippers in pre-Christian times in many parts of Europe despatched into the valley as the blazing symbols of the life-giving heavenly bodies. In many countries on the continent the lighting of bonfires at midsummer has been preserved. In the shortest night of the year they light up the mountain tops (in Switzerland this happens only on their national holiday on 1st August).

The midsummer festival in honour of the White Horse of Uffington died out in 1857. The luxuriant grass threatened to destroy once and for all the legendary figure until the Department of the Environment took over the responsibility for it. Now it is beautifully maintained.

There is no doubt that the gigantic White Horse is very old. But how old, nobody can say with certainty. Recognized experts in rock images believe that it dates from the period between 500 B.C. and the birth of Christ, as in style it very closely resembles the figures of the New Stone Age of the so-called La Tène culture, which originated with the Celts and was at that time very widespread in Europe. It was not able, however, to penetrate into the quite remote British Isles until the first few centuries after Christ. For this reason the White Horse possibly dates from this period.

The strange White Horse of Uffington is not the only gigantic chalk figure in the south of England. The town of Westbury in the county of Wiltshire lies where the Salisbury Plain runs down into the Vale of Pewsey. Not far from it, on the slope of Bratton Down, is the White Horse of Westbury (see ill. 83). There is evidence to show that in its present form it dates from the year 1778, but before this there was on the same site another, older white horse which did not have the

classical figure of the horse as seen today. In its shape the old horse closely resembled the remarkable horse at Uffington, and probably dates from the same period. Another piece of evidence to support its antiquity is the peculiar wall construction which, in the picture, is clearly discernible on the flat-topped hill above the White Horse. It dates from the Iron Age. Many archaeologists interpret it as an old fortification, but on how it was defended the archaeologists are silent.

The Iron Age fortification seems to have had some connection with the horse, as there is a similar wall-system on the hill at Uffington. In the immediate neighbourhood of other larger-than-life chalk figures there are similar installations.

One of the best known is Maiden Castle near Dorchester, not far from the south coast of England (see ill. 84). The huge installation is about 500 metres broad and one kilometre long and its origins perhaps go back as far as the New Stone Age. In any event it was used by the people of the Ice Age and continued in use until the Roman Conquest. Military experts have calculated that 250,000 men would have been required for the effective defence of such 'castles'. For this reason it is

83   In its present form the White Horse of Westbury in Wiltshire in England dates from 1778. But long before this there was a rock carving here which is said to have resembled the one in illustration 82. On the hill above the white horse there is a walled fortification dating from the Iron Age.

84   The largest installation of earthworks in England is Maiden Castle near Dorchester. It measures about 500 metres by 1,000 metres.

more than questionable whether Maiden Castle and the other such installations were ever fortifications or whether they were not much more likely to have been sanctuaries for pagan festivities.

Maiden Castle is certainly the biggest walled fortification dating from prehistoric times. So far no white figure has been discovered in its neighbourhood. But a few kilometres further north near Cerne Abbas there is the Giant Hill which again combines a wall system with a chalk figure. Here there is no horse but a gigantic figure of a god with a cudgel in his raised right hand (see ill. 85). Once more it is old traditional custom which seems to unravel the meaning both of the fortification on the peak of the hill and the gigantic human form, at the same time to confirm the spiritual link between the two: for centuries there had been a popular celebration on 1st May on the top of the hill inside the fortification. There young people used to erect a maypole around which they performed the age-old dances. The pagan May celebrations were in fact fertility rites and fertility was also distributed by the White Giant of Cerne Abbas whom some prehistorians consider to be Gog, an important figure in pre-Christian mythology. In the battle

against the pagan culture the Bible turned him into the ally of Satan in his struggle against Christ. But right into the past century this did not worry superstitious Englishwomen. They continued to believe in the magic powers of the old giant. If their marriages were childless they used to spend the night on the body of the giant and placed their hopes in its powers to bring fertility.

Another giant from the gentle hilly landscape of the south of England is the 'Long Man of Wilmington', who decorates the Windover Hill not far from Wilmington in Sussex. With his imposing height of 77 metres he must be the largest human form in the world. Aerial photographs show that also near him there are traces of walled fortifications. The English archaeologist T.C. Lethbridge interprets him as being a ritual figure of prehistoric sun-worshippers.

Naturally by no means all ancient chalk giants and white horses have been preserved until the present time. In the course of centuries most of them would have been made invisible by a green cover of grass. If in spite of this the trained eye of an archaeologist should detect new gigantic figures, it would be a rare piece of professional luck.

85   The Giant of Cerne Abbas does not look quite the same as it did in the year of its creation. It once had a cloak on its arm and next to it to the right, there stood a second large figure.

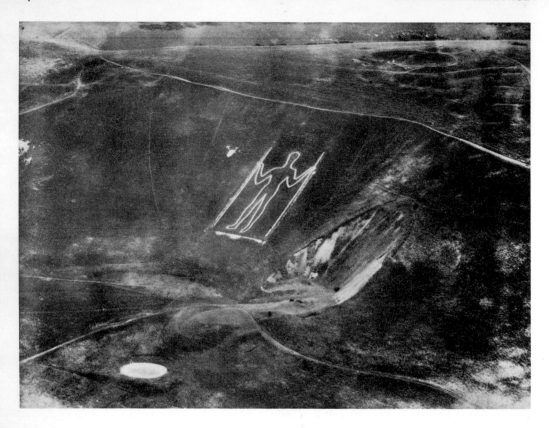

86 'The Long Man of Wilmington' is the world's largest picture of a human being. It measures 77 metres from head to toe. This aerial photograph shows that around him there must have been other lines than the two 'poles' which are to be seen in his hands.

In the 1950s Lethbridge embarked on a search for a giant who, according to old legends, was slumbering somewhere on the Gog-Magog hills close to the Iron Age camp near Wandlebury not far from Cambridge. This scholar was very surprised when he found not only him, but also two other human shapes, a horse which resembled the one at Uffington, and a triumphal chariot. One of the figures wielded a sword; Lethbridge believed that he was the mythological Wandil. Another figure could have been Gog or the Sun God. The third, a female figure, was identified by her discoverer as Magog or Epona, the old Gallic horse-goddess; it is 40 metres long. Lethbridge cleared a part of it and ventured to make an estimate of its age. He thought that the date of the Goddess was about 200 B.C., and the date of the horse and chariot the same, but in his opinion the date of the two male figures was about 150 years later. Unfortunately the site of the find has now completely run wild.

Another interesting discovery was made in 1963 by S.G. Wildman, as he was looking near Tysoe in the neighbourhood of Banbury in Warwickshire for a red horse which was said to have commemorated in 1461 the warlike horse of the Earl of

Warwick, perhaps in a place where the remains of a prehistoric horse were known to have been before. Wildman did not discover a horse but he found instead a rider with a whip or a rope in his hand, and a waterfowl, perhaps a goose, with raised head. And finally he also discovered an indefinable animal. Was it the red horse or a predecessor some thousand years older?

The English hill figures are full of mysteries. Their meaning has not been established with any certainty, nor has their huge size been satisfactorily explained. The fact that they are all best seen from the air, although their creators certainly had no opportunity to view them from that angle, excited wild speculations in the more imaginative. There are nothing more than a few bits of evidence to suggest whom or what these animals and human forms were intended to represent. It would appear that it was not present day Englishmen, but the prehistoric inhabitants of their island who were the first to have had the typical Anglo-Saxon sense of the extraordinary and the ludicrous.

The Gods with Hammer and Spear
Scandinavian scholars of rock carvings have a far easier task than their English colleagues. In Denmark, Sweden and Norway there are also horses and gods dating from centuries before the birth of Christ. In these countries too there are allusions to spring festivals with maypoles and dances dating from the pre-Christian era. Here too there are countless customs, legends and fairy stories which live on in the people. But everything is clearer and more comprehensible than in the British Isles. The reasons for this are the great number of find sites (16 in Denmark, 49 in Sweden, 81 in Norway) and their fine state of preservation. Moreover, in these countries most of the carvings have been cut deep into the rocks, and the recurring symbols which surround the figures of the gods carved on these rocks are straightforward and easy to interpret. There are figures which have a wheel for a body and hold a powerful spear. These represent the god Wotan, or, as he was called earlier, Ziu or Tyr. It cannot be any other god because the Nordic collection of legends, the Edda, describes him in eloquent terms in exactly the way he appears in the rock carvings. The famous spear of the old German god is called Gungnir. That too is recorded in the Edda.

Sceptics have protested that the famous collection of legends was committed to writing only around 1220 A.D., which would mean that they were about 2,000 years more recent than the rock carvings. However, Professor Herbert

Kühn meets the criticism with the remark that religious images live for thousands of years. Our churches produce pictures of Christ and the Madonna, and they lived nearly 2,000 years ago.

Even more convincing is the fact that the descriptions of the gods in the Edda are illustrated with the old pictures of Thor, the most powerful of Germanic gods. His symbols are the wheel divided into four and the hammer, and his sacred animal is the stag. This is exactly how the ancient Germanic peoples portrayed him in their rock carvings. His body is the four-spoked wheel, he swings the hammer high above his head which is often represented by the head of a stag (see ill. 44 and 87).

In the Edda the hammer of the god Thor is called 'Mjölnir', which means the one who crushes. Anyone who doubts that

87   The rock carving of Vitlycke near Tanum in the district of Bohuslän in Sweden is a ritual scene. The powerful figure of Thor is blessing a young couple.

such details as this description of the sacred hammer could really have been preserved in folklore for as long as nearly 20 centuries, which have elapsed between the execution of the rock carvings and the writing of the Edda, will be surprised to learn that many of the ancient Germanic images and customs are still alive today. He will also be surprised to learn that nearly every day he himself uses many of the names of the gods. It is not only the maypole that in some parts of Europe has been preserved till our times. In many places carpenters follow the old custom of dedicating a completed house with the old sacred hammer; the hammer which the auctioneer uses at auctions is also a symbolic representation of the sacred hammer. Until recently the blacksmith of Gretna Green performed marriages with this sacred implement.

Even now the descendants of the Germanic peoples are reluctant to eat horseflesh, because the horse was once a sacred animal, associated with the god Wotan (see ill. 88). The horse is represented to this day in the arms of the town of Hanover, and many other towns show the old wheel of Thor in their arms. The famous fleur de lys of royal France also can be traced back to the Nordic gods. It was the point of the blade of Wotan's sacred spear.

88 Horses were held in high esteem by the ancient Germanic people. They were the sacred animals of their god Wotan. The similarity in style of the animals in the rock decoration at Vitlycke near Tanum and that of the White Horse of Uffington is interesting to note.

Thursday took its name from the old Germanic storm god Donar, who was a predecessor of Thor. The English Thursday is derived from the German *Donnerstag* which was the day of Donar. Tuesday takes its name from the day of Ziu, or Tyr, because the letters Z and T are often interchangeable. Friday was the day dedicated to Frija, the wife of Wotan. The memory of people is so poor that they find it impossible to remember for more than hundreds or thousands of years things which were once sacred for them!

But to return to the Scandinavian rock carvings. One thing makes them easier for the scholars to understand as compared with the gigantic images in England. The dates of the images in Norway, Sweden and Denmark can be determined. Knives from the Bronze Age which were found near them, and later the 'winged swords', make this possible. Archaeologists are now able to distinguish pictures from two periods which run into each other: pictures from the Bronze Age between 1200 and 650 B.C. and those from the Iron Age (Hallstatt and La Tène cultures) between 650 B.C. and the beginning of Christian times. In the rock carvings dedicated to their gods by a sea-faring people, there were generally representations of ships or even whole fleets (see ill. 89). Then there was livestock, as they were an important means of livelihood for the predominantly cattle-breeding Germanic peoples; for

89   Ships are the subject of many rock pictures like this one drawn on a stone slab in Vitlycke near Tanum. The figures in the picture date from different periods. The oldest ones are the ships with crews represented only by small vertical lines. After 1,000 B.C. and more particularly around 500 B.C., human beings are portrayed as stylized figures. On the top right of the illustration, a man is shown wearing snow shoes.

them also the blessing of the gods was invoked by our ancestors (see ill. 90). About 98 A.D. the Roman historian Tacitus in his famous work on the Germanic peoples stated that their only and preferred form of wealth was livestock. Agriculture was not widely diffused and the image of the plough that occurs so frequently in the valleys round Mont Bego and in the Valcamonica has to date been found in only one place in Scandinavia (see ill. 90).

Despite all the trade links which existed in Europe in prehistoric times and despite all the cultural exchanges, in the last resort it was always its most personal history that each people recorded on the rocks of its native land. The documentation of the Germanic peoples is especially rich. Scandinavia is full of ancient images, and in spite of the impressive number of exhaustive scientific books on the finds, they have by no means all been committed to literature. For ambitious scholars of rock images there is work enough to keep them fully occupied for decades to come. Map 5 on page 265 gives an overall idea of the most important and most interesting places to visit.

90 At the excavation site Tegneby, near Tanum in the district of Bohuslän, archaeologists found an engraving which is unusual for northern Europe: a farmer with a team of oxen drawing a plough; a scene frequently found in southern Europe.

THE BIG STONES

'Dolmen', 'Menhirs' and 'Cromlechs'

More than 3,700 years ago the wife of Jacob, the biblical patriarch, died near Bethlehem. 'And Jacob set a pillar upon her grave: that is the pillar of Rachel's grave unto this day.' This is how the burial is described in *Genesis* (chapter 35 verse 20). 'Unto this day' – these words are still true. Rachel's grave in Palestine has survived unchanged all these thousands of years. The monumental gravestone which Jacob put up in honour of his dead wife has defeated the ravages of time.

The huge monument was in no way an exceptional gesture which only a man of high position could afford. The patriarch was merely performing a traditional act of homage rendered to their dead in the same way as did tens of thousands of surviving relatives. These great stone graves and ancestral memorials are called 'megaliths' by prehistorians. 'Mega' is the Greek prefix for 'great', 'lithos' in Greek means 'stone'. Nor was the Holy Land the only place where megaliths were erected. Our ancestors in Europe also put up countless of the same kind of stone monuments. In the last few centuries many of these have fallen to the plough or the bulldozer. In the Middle Ages others, as pagan shrines, were razed to the ground by the Christian Church, but thousands of them have been preserved: in Greece, Sicily, Sardinia, Corsica, the Balearic Islands, in northern Italy and in the southern

91 These huge 'tables' of stones weighing dozens of tons are the impressive dolmen, examples of which are to be found in almost all European countries. This is the dolmen of Calacuccia in Corsica.

92   *A small dolmen 11 kms west of Bourg-St. Andéol (Ardèche) in France.*

93   *The dolmen of Crucuno between Plouharnel and Erdeven in Brittany.*

94   Dolmen on the Île aux Moines in Brittany.

95   The 'Fairy Stone', a dolmen near Reignier some 15 kms south-east of Geneva.

96   The 'Stone of the Druids', a dolmen near Morschach, high above Lake Lucerne.

97 and 98   'Hunebedden' (barrows) in the Drenten area of eastern Holland.

99   *A small dolmen near Wilsede in the Lüneberger Heath in north Germany.*

100   Myrpold on Løjt near Abenra in Denmark.

101   The dolmen of Pentre Ifan in Wales.

102   Lanyon Quoit, a dolmen in Cornwall, England.

103   The Tarr Steps, locally known as the 'Devil's bridge', which cross the little river Barle near Winsford in Somerset in southwestern England. These stones are 3,000 years old and each one weighs 5 tons.

province of Apulia, in the south, north, and west of France, in Switzerland and Austria, in the southern, western and northern parts of Spain, in Portugal, the British Isles, Belgium, Holland, Denmark, in the north of Germany, and in the south of Scandinavia. There are also some examples in the countries on the southern shores of the Mediterranean from Libya to Morocco, including both Tunisia and Algeria.

Many of these prehistoric graves look like gigantic stone tables, made up of several supporting stones and a single great roofing slab which often weighs as much as 40 or 50 tons. They are called dolmen after an old Breton word which means a stone table (see ill. 91 to 92 and 104 to 110).

The earliest type of megalithic grave is the simple dolmen in the form of a table. A later development is the addition of a stone passage leading to the burial chamber (see ill. 111 to 113). In many instances the whole structure was covered with earth, the effect of which was to make artificial vaults (see ill. 114 to 116). In some cases the structure branched out in different directions and archaeologists occasionally found dozens of vaults in the side chambers. The final development was for the earth-covered burial chambers to form big

104 Dwarfie Stane, the 'dwarf stone' on Hoy in the Orkney Islands, is a megalithic grave of an unusual kind. This sandstone is about 9 metres long and hollow, and inside it 'beds' have been carved into the rock.

105 to 110   In addition to
illustrations 91 to 102,
these pictures are a further
selection of European
dolmen: 105   The Proleek
dolmen near Dundalk in
Ireland.

106   The dolmen of
Leganny near Castlewellan
in Northern Ireland.

107 *The Kemp stones near Dundonald in Northern Ireland.*

108 and 109 *The Cueva de Menga near Antequera in the Spanish province of Malaga.*

110   The dolmen of Soto near Trigueras in the Spanish province of Huelva.

111 to 116 *The passage graves are a later development of the simple dolmen. They consist of long passages covered with huge stone slabs. Occasionally the passages branch out. Examples of passage graves are also to be found in most European countries. 111 A passage grave behind a farmstead in the village of Mougau–en–Commana in the department of Finistère in Brittany. 112 'Hünenbett', one of more than four dozen passage graves in the Drentor area in eastern Holland.*

113   In England passage graves are called Long Barrows. This is a long barrow in West Kennet.

114   A passage grave covered with earth near Kleinenkneten not far from Wildeshausen in northern Germany.

115   *The passage grave of Waylands Smithy in the English county of Berkshire.*
116   *The burial chamber of a passage grave in the Troldøj near Stenstrup in Denmark.*

mounds, so-called tumuli, which could assume very large dimensions (see ill. 117 and 118). Among the largest tumuli was that of Barnenez on the peninsula of Kernéléhen in Brittany. This mound, which is 20 to 25 metres wide, 75 metres long, and 6 to 8 metres high, contains no less than eleven separate dolmen with long stone passages. Other examles of big tumulus graves in Brittany are the round tumulus of Tumlac en Arzon, which is 55 metres in diameter and 15 metres high, the Mont St. Michel near Carnac, which is 50 metres long and 10 metres high, and the tumulus of Gavrinis on the little island near Larmor-Plage, which is 60 metres in diameter. Even larger examples of such graves are the huge earth pyramids in the British Isles. The tumulus of New Grange in south-west Ireland is no less than 115 metres in diameter. The artificial mound of Silbury Hill near Marlborough is the largest megalithic structure in Europe (see ill. 119). It covers a surface of more than 2 hectares and is 45 metres high, and more than 4,700 years old. Many legends are linked with this strange hill, but to this day it has not given up its secret. Was it really a tumulus grave? So far British archaeologists have not been able to discover a single chamber in it.

117   The grave of Maes Howe: for 3,500 years this mound, consisting of clay and stones, eight metres tall, has stood near Stromness on the island of Orkney.

118   The burial chamber of Maes Howe. An impressive construction made from stone slabs.

119   Silbury Hill, as tall as a 17-storey house (43 m) occupying an area of five acres and 4,750 years old, is the largest prehistoric structure in Europe. The huge earthern cone rises out of the ground not far from Marlborough in Wiltshire.

The shapes of the megalithic structures are by no means limited to dolmen, passage graves, and gigantic mounds. Other examples of megalithic structures are upright stone columns, like the colossal monument of Champ Dolent in northern France (see ill. 5 on page 14) which, measuring 9.5 metres high and weighing more than 150 tons, is one of the biggest, or the Devil's Arrow near Borough Bridge in Yorkshire (see ill. 120 and 121). The scientific name of menhir for these stone columns comes like dolmen from the old Breton language – literally it means big stones. Frequently they do not stand separately but are aligned in long rows. Occasionally they are set out in the form of a circle or a large egg – then they are called cromlechs by the scientists, which means bent stones.

120   Near Boroughbridge in Yorkshire are to be found three 'Devil's Arrows'. The picture shows the most southerly stone which is no less than 7.5 metres tall.

Dolmen, menhirs, cromlechs: how foreign these words sound! Still more mysterious is the history of the big stones which lies behind these ancient Breton names. Scholars of megalithic culture are preoccupied by endless questions. How did our ancestors move these huge stones? At Locmariaquer, near Carnac in Brittany, the menhir which fell down and broke into several pieces, weighs 347 tons, exactly 40 tons more than a completely filled Boeing Jumbo Jet. It was 20.3 metres tall, taller in fact than a six-storey house. The highest stone column still standing, the menhir of Kerloas near Plouharnel in Brittany, weighs more than 150 tons; there is evidence that some 3,500 years ago our ancestors transported it for at least 2.5 kilometres before they stood it up. The famous megalithic sanctuary of Stonehenge, which amazes tourists by the size of the stones, is made of pieces of rock measuring up to eight metres in height and weighing up to 50 tons, which were transported nearly 230 kilometres from their quarry to the 'construction site'. The labour involved in transporting one piece of rock weighing 50 tons over a distance of 230 kilometres corresponds to what would be involved in transporting eight fully loaded buses without wheels over country paths. According to the calculations of scientists the erection of the supporting stones at Stonehenge would require the combined effort of 800 strong men. But the question of transporting the large stones is not the only mystery puzzling scholars. Examples of megaliths are to be found in nearly all western European countries, and in addition in Africa, Spain, Palestine, on the northern shore of the Black Sea, in the Arabian peninsula, and finally even in Tibet. Where was the cradle of this culture?

At first many archaeologists thought that it was the Mediterranean islands with their different megalithic struc-

121 The menhirs of Penrhos near Anglesey in Wales.

tures, about which more will be said later. However, these monuments are too recent to provide the source of other European megaliths; and the islands are themselves too small to be considered as possible birthplaces of the megalithic culture.

The megalithic idea must have come from a large country, a country through which nomadic peoples could have wandered and in which, honouring their ancestors they could have erected huge memorial stones, easily recognizable from a distance on hunting expeditions. Examples of this kind of memorial are erected in an endless stretch of land in the North African desert where tribes of the Marabout commemorate the ancient members of the tribe or Muslim sages with monumental gravestones. The Mediterranean islands could never have been the home of the megalithic civilization, however attractive this idea may have been at first sight.

Could the megalithic civilization have expanded from the Iberian peninsula where there are so many dolmen? For a long time the idea seemed worth exploring. Then another theory gained ground among the experts, which was widely accepted as having solved all the problems. It is set out in volume 2 of Professor Kühn's *Vorgeschichte der Menschheit* (*Prehistory of the Human Race*) in the following words: 'The great number of megalithic structures on the Mediterranean islands, on the Balearic islands, on Sardinia, Corsica, Malta, Gozo and in the whole of north Africa, point to the eastern Mediterranean, to an area where the two great cultures of Egypt and Mesopotamia were in continuous rivalry – Syria and Palestine. The idea that ancient Palestine must have been the starting point is reinforced by the discovery that Mesopotamia cannot boast of a single megalithic grave. In Egypt, on the other hand, obelisks and pyramids determine the shape of the landscape, but these are later developments and refinements of the megalithic idea. The genuine megalithic graves, the dolmen and passage graves built out of unpolished stone, do not exist in Egypt. In Palestine and Syria the original inhabitants were cattle breeders, nomads, but not agriculturalists. Cattle breeders look for grazing lands and large meadows, but also for hills and mountains as protection against aggressors and as suitable places for practising their religious cults. The fertile crescent of Syria and Arabia offered mountains and grazing lands, where the nomadic world flourished and has been able to survive to this day. Anyone travelling through the plains and valleys of Palestine and Syria can clearly see that only in this region was there sufficient space for this culture to succeed and later to expand to the west and to the north.'

Kühn described in detail the route by which the culture was diffused through Europe over a period of many centuries. 'The opening of new deposits of tin was the basic reason for the peoples of the Orient to colonize the Mediterranean area.' It was there that they first implanted their cultural heritage. Then the diffusion of the megalithic culture followed the maritime trade routes: '. . . along the north coast of Africa, to Spain, France, England, and Scandinavia – this was not a process of migration but rather of colonization. As the settlements were located on the coast, the stone graves are almost always to be found near the sea. It was rare for the bearers of the megalithic culture to move inland. Most of the Spanish examples of megalithic graves are to be found in the province of Andalusia. The reason is clear, this was the area which had mooring places for ships coming from the East, and it also had the richest deposits of silver and copper in all of Spain.' There is an overland trail of megalithic structures which runs from the south of France to the English Channel. Was it a short cut for the old maritime trade route which had to go round the Iberian peninsula? This theory fits well into the picture of the colonization of Europe by people of the megalithic culture. It is also reinforced by the fact that in Carnac in Brittany there are rows of stones which are identical to those in Gezer in Palestine, and that Egyptian pearls were found in the megalithic graves in Ireland.

Everything appears to fit perfectly. But despite the convincing character of Kühn's statement that a careful analysis of the finds confirmed the impressive picture of this first important stage of colonization, he points out elsewhere: 'Although most of the questions raised by this significant expansion of a culture have been solved in the last decades, the question of its place of origin still remains open.'

This was written in 1963. Since then, radio-active carbon dating, while throwing new light on the megalithic culture, has created new fundamental problems. If the colonization theory is valid the mégalithic culture must have gradually spread from the Mediterranean through Portugal and northern Spain to north-west France and the British Isles. However, the recent research done by Elizabeth Shee, the English archaeologist, on the oldest passage graves in Brittany (about 3900 B.C.; see ill. 113) has revealed them to be at least 750 years older than those in Portugal, and that the megaliths of southern Spain and the Mediterranean islands are more recent than the Portuguese. Elizabeth Shee writes: 'Unless earlier dates can be established for the Iberian peninsula it will be necessary to consider carefully whether the passage graves in Brittany are not actually the earliest megalithic graves in all the countries of Europe having an Atlantic coastline.'

Also many of the megalithic graves in the British Isles are considerably older than Professor Kühn assumed in 1963, when he wrote: 'In Great Britain all megalithic structures date from the Bronze Age; this was established by Abbé Breuil and Macalister.' Since then radio-active carbon dating has thrown up dates which go back to 2500 years B.C.

The origin of the big stones has again become obscure, and research into megalithic culture is faced with one more mystery, which at one time had seemed to be solved.

Astronomers Solve Archaeological Riddles

In the south of England near Salisbury in the county of Wiltshire huge stone columns, the largest of which are as tall as a three-storey house and weigh up to 50 tons, rise out of the flat landscape. Horizontal roofing slabs join together some of the upright columns to form colossal tors. Other roofing slabs have fallen down and it is clear that not all the supporting columns, which must have once belonged to the structure, are now standing. But even the ruins of the mighty structure are of an impressive size. Monumental, grandiose, timeless: these are the words that describe Stonehenge (see ill. 122).

122 (opposite) Stonehenge photographed on midwinter's day. The sun casts a ghostly light on the Stone Age sanctuary.

123 A reconstruction of the Sun Temple of Stonehenge, which shows what it might have looked like 3,500 years ago.

It is little wonder that the archaeologists of the 20th century were not the first to study this site which resembles a temple and looks as if in a time before time a race of giants had set up its columns. Early in the 17th century, the interest of the English king James I was aroused by Stonehenge. The king sent his court architect, Inigo Jones, to study the mysterious ruins and to establish how old the structure was. The architect reported that the ruins were the remains of a Roman temple. About 50 years later King Charles II sent John Aubrey, who was supposed to be well versed in antiquities, to examine the stones of Stonehenge. This scholar had previously written about a very similar but less impressive site, the stone circles of Avebury. Perhaps he would also be able to unravel the mystery of Stonehenge. Aubrey examined the stones with care and came to the conclusion that Stonehenge was a Druid sanctuary. Druid was the name given to the priests of the Celts in Britain and Gaul. They were supposed to be able to read the stars and to foretell natural events by examining the intestines of animals and observing the flight of birds. Highly educated, they occupied high political and judicial offices and were most important as teachers of the young. In the works of Roman historians, particularly Julius Caesar, there was much about the achievements of the Druids. Who else could have been the builders of Stonehenge?

This seemed to be a satisfactory explanation to the origins of the inscrutable stones. When, at the beginning of the 19th century, the English scholar William Stukeley drew a new ground plan of Stonehenge, he was also convinced that he was dealing with a Druid structure. He was reinforced in this belief by an important discovery. 80 metres from the altar stone, which was a piece of rock in the centre of the stone circles, there was a large single stone, the heel stone. If anyone looked at the heel stone from the altar stone in the early morning on midsummer's day he would see the sun rise above it. Was this a mere chance? Surely not, because the Druids were known of old for their study of the stars. In the 18th and 19th centuries a kind of mania for everything Celtic had swept over the whole of Europe. Anything of uncertain origin was at once ascribed to the Celts and anything which was puzzling or obscure was thought to be the work of the Druids. Many dolmen in the Alpine region, such as the one on a small hill commanding a good view above the bobsleigh run of St. Moritz, are popularly referred to as 'dolmen stones'. When at the end of the last century archaeologists discovered that by no means all pre-Roman remains owed their origin to the Celts and their priests, the true meaning of the big stones of

Stonehenge was again open to question. Once more scientists began their search for a satisfactory answer to the problem of their antiquity. In 1901 an official astronomer, Sir Norman Lockyer, produced the first concrete result. He said himself that if the theory is correct that the builders of Stonehenge used the line from the altar stone to the heel stone for measuring the altitude of the sun on the longest day of the year then this whole system for taking bearings can only be approximately valid today. The course of the earth round the sun changes very slightly over periods of hundreds and thousands of years and this necessarily results in some variation. On the other hand the change in course can be calculated exactly and it should therefore be possible to calculate precisely when the system of taking bearings had functioned accurately. This would be when a priest saw the sun rising exactly over the middle of the heel stone, as he observed it from the middle point of the altar stone. The result of Lockyer's calculation was that this would have happened in the year 1680 B.C. with a possible margin of error of plus or minus 200 years. In 1935 Herbert Stone repeated the calculation on the basis of even more precise measurements taken from both stones and came to the conclusion that the year was 1840 B.C. This proved that Stonehenge was built before the age of the Celts because they did not appear in Britain until about 250 B.C.

Was this not a contradiction in itself? The calculations of the astronomers Lockyer and Stone rested on the assumption that the sun watchers had erected the stones of Stonehenge on the exact spots where they now stand. And the results of the calculations led back to a period when there were certainly no Druids versed in astronomy. The professional world, however, doubted the accuracy of the calculation.

There was yet another argument which spoke against the excessive antiquity of the gigantic construction. In 1923 the source of the big stones was successfully identified. They came from Pembrokeshire in south Wales, no less than 230 kms from Stonehenge. How was it possible to have solved such an unusual transportation problem thirty-seven and a half centuries ago? Excitement mounted as the process of radio-active carbon dating made it possible to put an exact date on the mysterious prehistoric temple. In 1649 Aubrey had discovered around the structure of the temple a circle of 56 deep holes which had been filled with limestone and charcoal immediately after they had been dug. The radio-active carbon test was carried out on one of these holes. The result was sensational! The answer was 1847 B.C. with a possible variant of 275 years. This was just seven years short of the result obtained by Dr. Stone's calculation based on astronomy! Stonehenge really was older than the Druids and into the bargain it was definitely a place from which calculations could be made to measure the distance of the sun.

This puzzling discovery brought Dr. G.S. Hawkins, the American astronomer, onto the project. He systematically began to attack the problem of the old temple from the starting-point that Stonehenge was after all built out of more than two stones. Perhaps the bearings which were significant from the point of view of astronomy depended on more than the connecting line between the altar and heel stones. Hawkins again measured all the stones of the structure and drew on his charts 7,140 possible connecting lines. He fed into a computer the bearings of these lines in order to find out whether any particular ones occurred more frequently than was to be expected according to the laws of probability. This in fact was the case. Did the measurements which were discovered throw a new light on possible astronomical phenomena? In order to establish this it was necessary for Hawkins to calculate to which declinations the figures obtained did in fact correspond.

The declination is an important concept in finding the position of a celestial object. A line drawn between a celestial object and the middle point of the earth would penetrate the earth's surface at a precise point. The geographic latitude of this point is identical with the declination of the celestial object. The degrees of two such declinations can be calculated for each siting line established between two stones, depending on whether the observer takes his bearings from stone A or stone B.

Hawkins' computer discovered that at Stonehenge the declinations $\pm 29°$, $\pm 24°$, and $\pm 19°$ were the most frequent. This was an exciting result, as around the year 1880 B.C. the declination of the sun at the time of the summer solstice was $+24°$ and the declination at the time of the winter solstice was $-24°$. The moon goes through four extreme positions on its rather more complicated route. Around 1800 B.C. these were $+29°$, $-29°$, $+19°$, and $-19°$!

Hawkins had thrown light on the mystery of Stonehenge. Or could it all have been a matter of chance? The computer whirred again. This time it calculated the probability with which any arrangement of exactly the same number of stones as stand in Stonehenge would give by chance the same alignments with declinations of $\pm 29°$, $\pm 24°$, and $\pm 19°$. The result was 1:1,000,000. There could be no more talk of chance.

Stonehenge was indeed an old sun and moon sanctuary.

But Hawkins was not yet satisfied with his discoveries. Reconstructions showed a picture into which more could be read than the relative positions of one stone to another. There was the so-called sarsen circle, the circle consisting of big supporting stones, which joined together above it a row of lintels. In addition, in the centre there were five even bigger triliths, composed of three stones and looking like cyclopean tors. Then there were the 56 mysterious holes round the temple discovered by Aubrey and since then called after him, the Aubrey holes. What did they all mean?

The big triliths and sarsen circle soon gave up their secrets; if a priest looked from the inner courtyard of the structure through one of the inner tors, in such a way as to be looking at the same time through a particular tor of the sarsen circle, then according to the combination of the inner and outer tor he would have a precise point in the skies in view, which corresponded to one of the already known declinations ($\pm 29^\circ$, $\pm 24^\circ$, $\pm 19^\circ$).

The Aubrey holes did not give up their secrets so easily and perhaps it will never be possible to say with certainty whether the explanation which Hawkins had found, and which he considered to be 'plausible', really went to the root of the matter. In any event the American astronomer's theory is extremely exciting.

The holes could not have served as points from which bearings were taken. Hawkins considered them as useful aids in making calculations. He assumed that in prehistoric times the priest placed six yardsticks into the holes clockwise, with a stick in each of the 10th, 19th, 28th, 38th, 47th, and 56th holes. Every year the priest would move the yardsticks forward by one hole. By this simple method of calculation they were able to predict within a few days the dates of solar and lunar eclipses. For example, whenever a yardstick was put into a hole on the line between the altar and heel stones it was possible to predict an eclipse of the sun at the time of the winter solstice. By this method it was possible to know the approximate times of eclipses. According to Hawkins it would then be possible to discover the exact day marking with a stone or stick placed in front of one of the thirty tors of the sarsen circle and then removing the stone or stick back one tor every day. When this 'moon stick' was between the 30th and the first of the pillars, in fact aligned again with the straight line drawn between the altar and heel stones, then there could be an eclipse of the moon on that day insofar as this alignment was confirmed by one of the yardsticks in the Aubrey holes. If the moon stick was exactly on the opposite side of the sarsen circle, an eclipse of the sun could be expected.

To many scientists Hawkins' theory appeared improbable. They countered with the question, how could prehistoric man have had such a deep knowledge of astronomy? But this objection can easily be met. Were not our ancestors thousands of years ago closer to events in the starry heavens than people of the 20th century who very seldom see the stars, let alone observe them? And did not the daily and yearly path of the sun affect their everyday lives, conducted in natural surroundings, more closely than ours? The most recent discoveries of the English astro-archaeologist Professor Thom are so eloquent that it is no longer possible to doubt the elaborate astronomical observations of our early ancestors. Why then was Hawkins' theory about the Aubrey holes considered so improbable?

Professor Thom was fascinated by the results which the computer had thrown up to show that Stonehenge was a centre of astronomy but these results did not satisfy him. If the most famous of all British prehistoric sanctuaries was a calendrical centre, why could not the thousands of megalithic circles and rows of stones and single menhirs, which exist in the British Isles, not have been the same (see ill. 124 and 125)?

124   In many places in the British Isles there are examples of prehistoric circles of stone, such as these near Beaghmore in the county of Tyrone, Northern Ireland.

125 *The stone circle of Drombeg near Glandore in County Cork, Ireland.*

This thought haunted him. So he proceeded to investigate no less than 450 stone structures and used the most modern surveying instruments to make accurate plans of more than half of them. Combined with plans which were already in existence, Professor Thom had, in the end, sufficient material to feed a computer with the dates of about 600 megalithic structures from all over the British Isles. The results of the calculations were a rich reward for his detailed and pains-taking work. Thom was able to establish with certainty·58 alignments to the sun and 23 to the moon. 50 further alignments to the sun and 15 to the moon were established as very probable, and 10 to the sun and 4 to the moon as possible.

But that was not the only result. The computer discovered that in addition to these alignments there were a number of preferred directional lines which could not have been used for measuring directions of the sun, or moon. Thom studied them closely and discovered that the builders of the megalithic monuments must have observed very accurately the paths of the bright fixed stars among them Capella (with 12 certain and 3 probable alignments of the stones), Deneb (with 5 certain and 2 probable), Arcturus (with 3 certain and 5 probable), Castor (with 3 certain and 4 probable), Spica (with 3 certain and one probable), Antares and Altair (each with 2 certain and 3 probable), Pollux (with 2 certain and one probable), Procyon (with one certain and 2 probable), and Vega (with one certain and one probable).

While, for instance, the stone circles of Castle Rigg (see ill. 126) and Long Meg (see ill. 127) were sun and moon observatories, from the Rollright Stones (see ill. 128) in Oxfordshire, in addition to measuring distances to the sun, it was possible to observe and to take measurements of Deneb (see ill. 129 and 130), the brightest star in the constellation of the Swan. It was probable that Avebury in Wiltshire, the next most important and extensive stone structure after Stonehenge, permitted bearings to be taken on the star Deneb.

What has had to be compressed into a few sentences here, as the outcome of many years of pioneering work, is described with scientific precision by Professor Thom in his book *Megalithic Sites of Britain*. In this book he states that our ancestors nearly 4,000 years ago must have had a most accurate solar calendar. Alignments which were fixed by definite points in the movement of the sun indicate that the

126 to 130   In England and Scotland as well as in Ireland there are a great number of prehistoric stone circles. These pictures show a selection. 126   The circle of Castlerigg in the hills near Keswick in Cumberland consists of 38 stones.

127 'Long Meg and her Daughters' are the names given by the local population to another group of stone circles in Cumberland.

128 The Rollright Stones, a group of stone circles near Gloucester.

129   After Stonehenge, the circles of Avebury are the most important stone structure in Great Britain.

builders of the megalithic structures must have divided the year into 16 nearly equal periods, 'months' of 23, 23, 24, 23, 23, 23, 23, 22, 22, 22, 22, 23, 23, 23, 23, and 23 days. The year of the megalithic peoples consisted, like our own year, of 365 days, and it also had every fourth year a leap year's day which was only inserted into our calendar 15 centuries later, in the time of Caesar. Professor Thom made exhaustive calculations to prove that the best solution to the problem of numbering the days of a 16 months' year which started on the day of the vernal equinox was to follow definite astronomical positions.

The big stones in the British Isles were then not merely gravestones. They were at the same time carefully sited centres of observation and rituals connected with the calendar. But what was the position of the megalithic monuments in the other countries of Europe? Did they also have such profound significance from the point of view of astronomy?

130 *This structure must once have been of a vast size as is shown by this picture of a reconstruction.*

Avenues of Stones

The old fishing village of Carnac in the south west of Brittany lies at the point where the Quiberon peninsula begins to jut out into the sea. The traveller who leaves Carnac to the north along the road D119 and bears to the north east along the road D196, after a few kilometres will come to a picturesque stretch of land covered with pine woods smelling of resin with big expanses of heather and gorse. Suddenly on the left there appears a most remarkable sight: hundreds of large stones standing up like stooks of hay in a large field – the menhirs of Kermario (see ill. 131). The largest of them stand a good 4

131   The menhirs of Kermario consist of 1,029 stone columns aligned in ten parallel rows . . .

metres high. A closer inspection soon reveals what cannot be immediately seen from the road. The menhirs are not distributed at random over the landscape, but they are aligned in long rows. Over a distance of more than a kilometre there are ten of these rows which are nearly parallel. Anyone who makes the effort to count the stones will find that they total 1,029.

Exactly half a kilometre further to the east, the astonished motorist will be met by another sight which should give him reason to stop. Here, in the middle of the moor, appearing out of the gorse and heather are a further 594 menhirs; 39 of them form a wide semi-circle, the remaining 555 are aligned in 13 almost parallel rows 880 metres long. This is the menhir field of Kerlescan (see ill. 132).

132 . . . another 594 stones, the menhirs of Kerlascan, are close by.

If the motorist, instead of driving further eastwards, had turned into the narrow road D196, which crosses the D119 from Carnac, and driven further to the west, after a few hundred metres he would have met a similar view: 1,099 big menhirs in eleven rows nearly 1,200 metres long and 70 upright stones which form a big semi-circle. This is Ménec.

Those who want to see even more should drive back to Carnac following the Route Nationale 781 to the north-west. Eight kilometres along this road are the upright stones of Kerzerho which consist of 129 menhirs aligned in ten rows.

In other parts of Brittany there are smaller or less well preserved fields of the same kind, and the traveller in this ancient land will come across single rows of stones at nearly every turn. One of the most picturesque of these single rows is that of Lagatjar on a frequently windswept plain near Camaret which is situated on an inlet of the sea opposite Brest (see ill. 133).

It is easy to believe that these strange rows of stones would make particularly good observation lines to the sun or other celestial bodies, and many investigations have been undertaken on this basis. However, the archaeologists ran into several problems. On the one hand the taking of accurate measurements on the three big menhir fields around Carnac was hardly possible because many of the stones had fallen

133   In the far north-west of France the menhirs of Lagatjar emerge in a long row from a treeless plain.

down, and in some cases, at one time or another, had been re-erected at random, with the result that some of the rows are no longer properly aligned.* On the other hand it became clear at each site that instead of running parallel to each other the lines of menhirs started from more or less well preserved semi-circles and gently separated as they took slightly different directions. Therefore each row points in a different direction and in the end the long rows of stones prove in practice to be far less suited as observation lines than had at first been assumed. It was much easier to take bearings along the avenues formed by two rows standing next to each other. In order to get a good sighting line to a distant point, an alignment of more or less one kilometre is needed. In the same way as a row of houses along both sides of a straight street appear to meet at the end, so also do the two lines of menhirs along each of the avenues of stones.

Although the menhir fields would seem in the main to point towards the position of sunrise and sunset at the time of the spring and autumn equinoxes, this could apply at most to one or two of the rows of menhirs which gradually fan out. The German astronomer, Professor Rolf Müller, in his publication in 1970 *The Sky above Stone Age Man* gave what sounded like a very plausible explanation. Professor Müller writes about the rocks of Kerlescan as follows: 'According to

* Most of these stones are easily recognized. They have a small hole immediately above ground level which is filled with pink coloured concrete.

my measurements and calculations it would appear that if the slope of the land which rises from the south-east to the north-west is taken into account, the northern row is directed to a point on the horizon where the midsummer sun sets. The way the base lines between the equinoxes and the solstices fan out leads to the assumption that they were used to determine calendar dates lying between them in the summer calendar months.' Professor Müller calculated the deviation from the sun of three specially selected rows of stones at Kerlescan. The results fit perfectly into his theory that Kerlescan was a gigantic stone calendar. When tried out it gave dates which also fitted the Megalithic Age sixteen-month calendar used in the British Isles. The professor wrote: 'This is an interesting discovery but it is important to point out that it leaves much to be desired from the point of view of accuracy. It would be an easy matter to clarify the question further if one could find out either the original measurements which lay behind the photograph of the plan (from which Müller worked) or take the trouble to measure on the site the distances between as many as possible of the stone columns. We owe it to the research of megalithic structures to find a solution to the problem, especially as no other place offers the opportunity to take so many measurements. Brittany is certainly worth a journey.'

This was in 1970. Since then, the 70-year-old Professor Thom, who had devoted 30 years of his life to megalithic structures in Great Britain, undertook a journey to Brittany with a complete team of scientists and surveyors. In a documentary film about his life's work which was made in 1975 he told Magnus Magnusson, a BBC television producer, that the expectations with which he had gone to Brittany had been completely fulfilled.

Long rows of menhirs in many parallel lines are peculiar to north-western France and the British Isles. Double rows of big stones, on the other hand, are common, also in northern Germany. It is true that the menhirs there are not of outstanding quality but the character of the long avenues is unmistakable. The north German stone graves always have subterranean chambers and huge roofing slabs. Most of the examples of these barrows are to be found on the Lüneburger Heath to the south of Hamburg and the Ahlhorner Heath near Wildeshausen to the south-west of Bremen. These megalithic structures also date from approximately 2000 and 1700 B.C., in other words from the New Stone Age. Between them there are hundreds of small barrows and extended cemeteries dating from the later Bronze Age.

(134) *(135)*

(136) *(137)*

The most important barrows in the Lüneberger Heath are the seven stone structures near Fallingbostel which lies in the middle of an army training area, and as a result can only be visited on Sundays and official holidays, and the big grave centre of Kleckerwald not far from the little village of Buchholz (see ill. 134). In the Ahlhorner Heath there are five big stone structures which have survived for thousands of years: the 'Visbeker bride' and the 'Visbeker bridegroom' which according to an old tradition should only be visited at night, the Glaner Braut, the Hohen Steine, and the Kleinenknetener Stones (see ill. 135 to 137).

The theory that the north German barrows indicated important points in the sun calendar is not exactly new. As early as the summer of 1935 Professor Müller took measurements of the stones on the Ahlhorner Heath to confirm or contradict this theory. The Visbeker bridegroom is directly in line with the sunrise or sunset at the time of the equinox; the Visbeker bride pointed to the exact spot where the moon went down on midsummer's day 3,750 years ago, the Kleinenknetener Stones and the Hohen Steine clearly indicate dates in the sixteen months' sun calendar year. The Glaner Braut seems to have been a place from which to observe the moon.

It is relatively easy for modern astro-archaeologists to take measurements of the old stone observatories and to establish their significance. They have at their disposal precision instruments and accurate theodolites with which they can take bearings. The measurements must indeed be exact to confirm valid dates. A measurement mistake of only half a degree of an angle can make a date doubtful or even impossible. If precise measurements are available calculations can begin. These call for professional qualifications in mathematics and geometry which are beyond the layman. Hence the fierce quarrel which has broken out among archaeologists. Some of them are completely sceptical about the astronomical significance of the megaliths, others, who understand the evidence which mathematical calculations can provide, reproach their colleagues because they only question the calculations of the astro-archaeologists because they do not understand them. This quarrel is very much alive, and will only cease when those experts who refuse to look beyond the boundaries of their traditional fields, are dead.

But does not the very existence of those sceptics, who do not comprehend mathematical relationships, provide a powerful argument against the astronomical significance of the megalithic structures? If 20th century people with

134 to 137 (opposite) Barrows in north Germany. Long stone avenues enclose burial chambers which are covered with flat stones. Among the most important of these graves are:

134 The graves of Kleckerwald, south of Hamburg.

135 The Visbeker Bride near Wildeshausen, the last few stones of which form a line of sight.

136 The Kleinenknetener stones south of Wildeshausen.

137 The Visbeker Bridegroom, which measures 115 metres and is the longest barrow in north Germany.

specialist training cannot understand the architecture of the ancient structures, how then could people of the Stone Age who quite clearly were not even able to write, have constructed those elaborate stone monuments with such extraordinary precision some 40 centuries ago? The question of how they did it still awaits a solution, but that they did it is now beyond doubt. People of the New Stone Age did in fact possess an extremely precise knowledge of geometry.

Mathematicians and Engineers of the Stone Age

A people able to build stone observatories of finite precision must have been able to measure on site the distances between two stones, the diameter of a circle of stones, the distance between different circles of stones. They must have been able to use some accurate system of measurement and may even have had some unit of distance like the metre. If they had such a unit, Professor Thom said to himself, it must be possible to find out how long it was. With the persistence and tenacity typical of a Scottish scholar, he set about solving this question. He carefully measured hundreds of upright stones, developed mathematical methods which helped him to comprehend their installations even in cases where single stones had sometimes fallen away or been dislodged by growing trees or by the movements of the earth, or where only a few stones still survived.

Years of fieldwork were coupled with comprehensive statistical analyses, mathematical comparisons, and calculations of possible margins of error. And one day the answer was there: the men of the New Stone Age had throughout the British Isles used one unit of measurement which Thom called MY, the Megalithic Yard. It was the equivalent of 82.9 centimetres and within Great Britain the variations never measured more than a few millimetres.

The term megalithic yard used by Thom was derived from the unit of measurement in general use in England at the time, the yard*. This is of linguistic interest: the word 'yard' originally meant a wooden rod or stick. In this form our ancestors could well have carried a unit of measurement similar to our ruler or tape-measure. The ruler is now somewhat out of fashion but it is still used in the schoolroom.

The French word 'verge' for the old French unit of measurement means exactly the same thing: wooden rod or stick. And the Spanish term 'vara' has the same linguistic origin. The vara is an ancient measure which was used over the entire sphere of Spanish cultural influence. The Conquistadors took it with them to the New World. The vara

* 1 yard = 0.9144 metre.

was not of exactly the same length everywhere in the Spanish Empire. In the course of time here and there small variations occurred within this vast empire. The vara in Madrid measured 83.6 cm, in Burgos 84.3 cm, in Peru 83.8 cm. The average was 84.0 cm which was only 11 mm longer than the Megalithic Yard. This showed that a unit of measurement originating in the Stone Age had survived well into historic times almost unchanged for thousands of years.

If this is correct then the unit of measurement of the Stone Age must have been known on the continent of Europe as well as in the British Isles. Again it was Professor Müller, the German astronomer, who was the first to find confirmation on the continent of what Thom had discovered in England. He carried out measurements on the stone circles at Odry on the Tuchel Heath in what was formerly west Prussia. The measurements of ten diameters of different circles and sixteen spaces between different circles led the scientist to an exact unit of measurement of 82.7 cm in his calculations. That differs by only 2 mm from the megalithic yard discovered by Thom. More than 1,000 km away from the British Isles the people of the Stone Age had constructed megalithic circles according to the same units of measurement as those in the regions which are present-day England and Scotland. Furthermore as Thom and his team recently carefully measured megalithic structures in Brittany, he found everywhere the same unit of length, the megalithic yard. The nearly incredible unity of measurements in Scotland, Wales, west Prussia and Brittany, the occasional deviations of only a few millimetres led to a most interesting conclusion. Somewhere in Europe there must have been a central 'office of weights and measures' which delivered wooden rulers to different parts of the continent. If each community had obtained its ruler not from a central point but from a neighbouring village the errors in length would certainly then have been far greater.

In the megalithic circles which Thom had investigated the diameters were nearly always a multiple of the megalithic yard. There were stone circles with diameters of 4, 7, 8, 11, 12, 15 and so on to 105, 125, and 137 megalithic yards (MY). With diameters based on these numbers the geometric result was that the circumferences of the circles could always be divided by 2.5 MY. That fact appeared to be very important to our ancestors in making these constructions, because whenever they chose a diameter which did not lead to this result, as for instance of 5, 6, 9, 10, 13, 14 and so on MY, they made the circles a little bigger, with the result that there was a compromise between an almost integral numbered diameter and

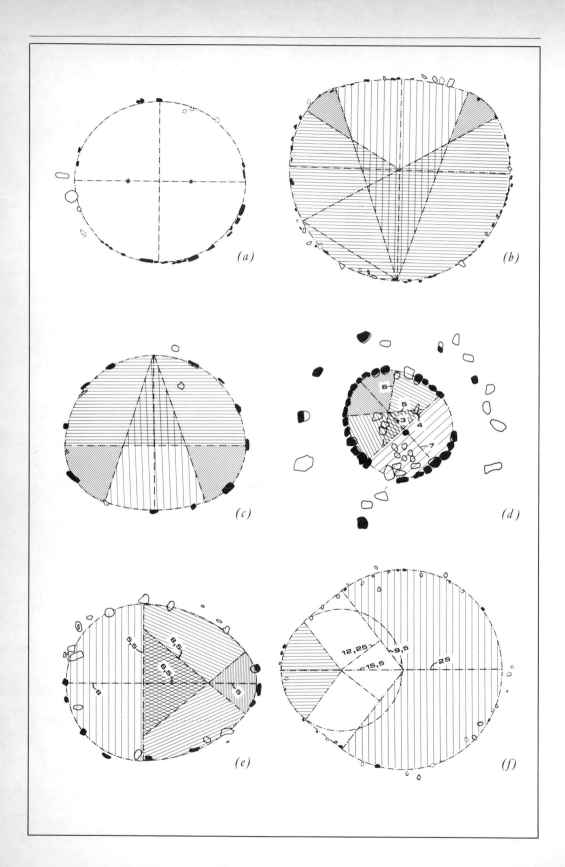

(a)

(b)

(c)

(d)

(e)

(f)

a circumference which was a multiple of 2.5 MY. However, many of the prehistoric stone circles were not true circles, but elipses or egg-shaped, which could be divided into groups of quite different shapes. After a labour of many years Thom was able to unravel the means of construction which were the bases of the plans for these circular structures. They revealed very considerable skills in geometry. Illustrations 138a to f show the main forms and the subsidiary lines which are required to support their construction. The figures in the diagrams give the measurements in MY. The shaded wedge-shaped parts are segments of circles. The top ends of the wedges are the central points of the arcs of the circles which can be drawn round the wedges.

In the construction of the egg-shapes right-angled triangles constantly recur, for example in figure 'd' the triangle with sides of 3, 4, and 5 MY, in the figure '3' the triangle with sides of $5\frac{1}{2}$, $6\frac{1}{2}$, $8\frac{1}{2}$ MY and in the figure 'f' the one with sides of $9\frac{1}{2}$, $12\frac{1}{4}$ and $15\frac{1}{2}$ MY. This triangle is exactly the one which is known in the school text-books as the triangle of Pythagoras. Our mathematicians have called it after the Greek scholar and philosopher Pythagoras whose disciples are thought to be the discoverers of this geometric phenomenon. Masons still construct right angles today on the basis of the ancient principle with a piece of string which is divided into three lengths of 3, 4, and 5 metres.

If the people of the Stone Age had knowledge of the so-called Pythagorean triangle, did the Greeks for their part discover it again, or did they resume an intellectual heritage 1,500 years old? Diodorus Siculus, the Greek historian who came from Sicily and was a contemporary of Julius Caesar, told of a big island to the north of France, the Kingdom of the mysterious 'Hyperboreans'. He describes a large round stone temple on this distant island and writes: 'It is also said that God visits the island every 19 years at the time the stars return to their starting points in the constellation; for this reason the period of 19 years is called a Metonic cycle'. Diodorus goes on to describe the astronomical measurements in Stonehenge where the 56 Aubrey holes enclose three cycles of exactly 18.61 years. Diodorus named the cycle of about 19 years a Metonic Cycle after the Greek astronomer Meton who proposed a similar period about 432 B.C. He gives credit to a fellow countryman who did not really deserve it. In his *Historic Library* Diodorus extols the outstanding mathematical competence of the Hyperboreans and says that the scholars of this people transmitted their knowledge to the Greeks. Did the followers of Pythagoras inherit his famous

138 The prehistoric stone 'circles' are not always real circles. There are some which are exact ellipses, a: Sands of Forvie, 57° 19′ 6″/1° 58′ 8″ (p. 183); various flattened circles; b: Dinnever Hill, 50° 35′ 4″/4° 38′ 8″ and c: Bar Brook, 53° 16′ 6″/1° 34′ 9″), cleverly constructed 'eggs'; d: Druid Temple, 57° 27′ 4″/4° 11′ 4″ and e: Allan Water, 55° 20′ 8″/2° 50′ 1″) and finally, circles which are pieced together, f: Barrowstone Rig. 55 46′ /2° 42′). The stones marked black are still in their original sites, the other stones have either fallen or have been re-erected. The areas with hatch lines indicate segments of circles. The figures mentioned indicate lengths in megalithic yards.

theorem, in the same way as Meton may have inherited his vast knowledge of astronomy, directly from the descendants of the Old Stone Age Britons? No precise evidence will ever be forthcoming to prove this.

Mysterious Ornaments

It is true that no exact date can be put on the transition from the Stone to the Bronze Age, and it is also true that the metal did not appear everywhere in Europe at the same time, but one thing is certain today, the big megaliths of the British Isles, Spain, and Brittany go back to an era when Bronze was still unknown to the human race. In not a single passage grave in England, Scotland, or Ireland were any metal objects found among the original burial gifts which relatives or friends gave to their dead to accompany them on their journey into the other world.

But the supporting and roofing stones of many of the burial chambers are often thickly covered with mysterious decorations. The lines are cut deep into the stone without the use of any metal tools. The architects of prehistoric times must, with enormous effort, have chiselled them with flintstone onto the pillars and columns of their cyclopean structures. There were often zigzag lines, diamond shapes and spirals; sometimes also sun or flower-like symbols, circles or simple parallel lines. Nearly every grave had its own peculiar style or points of detail although they were all similar in their general features. The passage graves in eastern Ireland, between Dublin and the river Boyne, are particularly rich in this kind of engraving. In the valley of the Boyne itself are to be found the famous New Grange (see ill. 139 and 140) and Knowth (see ill. 141); about 25 kms to the south-east is the Fourknocks (see ill. 142).

In England there are 55 such passage graves with deeply incised engravings. The most important are Dod-Law, Old-Bewick and Roughting Linn, all of which are in Northumberland. In these graves cup forms and concentric circles predominate in the same way as those to be found on many rocks throughout Europe.

The most famous Scottish stone grave with carvings is Achnabreck (ill. 71 and 72). But perhaps the most interesting is an unusual discovery in 1860 made by Scottish archaeologists in a grave near Towie in the county of Aberdeenshire. They found round stones, the size of tennis balls, which were completely covered with engravings of spirals, angles, serpentine lines and concentric circles. The surface of these balls had been carved away to form four button-like circles before being engraved (see ill. 144).

139 to 143   On the walls of the megalithic graves there are often symbolic engravings, spirals, circles, wavy or zigzag lines and other patterns. The illustrations show a few examples from Ireland and England. 139/140 (opposite) A spiral decoration in the huge passage grave of New Grange in County Meath in eastern Ireland.

141 *Geometric signs on a stone in the passage grave of Knowth, County Meath.*

142 *Zigzag designs on a porch stone from the grave at Fourknocks, also in County Meath.*

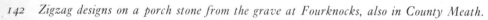

143 *Stone engravings on the burial chamber of Bryn-Celli-Ddu in Anglesey.*

144 *Stone balls covered with decorations are amongst the most remarkable finds from the megalithic graves in Scotland.*

What is the meaning of these strange decorations on the walls of these large graves, on the mysterious stone balls of Towie, and on the other small stone objects which, judging by their shapes, could not have been in general use? Many scientists believe that these figures had a ritual significance or were sacred symbols. The attribution to the realm of myth or religion of everything which to us appears incomprehensible or devoid of practical purpose is a facile solution. But nevertheless this concept may be particularly appropriate in this case. Would people at the end of the Stone Age have given themselves such endless trouble and worked so carefully on stone with stone, if they had not been spurred on by an inner, driving force which gave them the required tenacity and patience? This kind of compulsive desire for self-expression is nearly always inspired by religious concepts.

But there have been other attempts to find the answer to the question 'why?' Among the experts in megalithic culture, two prominent astronomers, Professor Thom of Scotland and Professor Müller of Germany, suspect that there are astronomical implications in some of the engravings on the megalithic stone graves. Thom is not certain of their meaning but he believes that these shapes, especially the cup forms and the circles, will one day give up their secrets and clearly reveal the intellectual world of mathematicians and astronomers in prehistoric times. In his attempts to find the meaning of these engravings Müller had several concrete examples in mind, such as the mysterious lines with curved endings which are carved on the megalithic grave of Locmariaquer near Carnac in Brittany known as the 'Table des Marchands' (see ill. 145). This huge dolmen was erected so that it pointed in the direction of the sunrise on midsummer's day, which indicates that the builder had a considerable knowledge of astronomy. Professor Müller believes: '. . . that the signs on this most interesting supporting stone of the passage grave of the "Table des Marchands" refers to particular dates in the trajectory of the moon and to eclipses both of the moon and the sun.' He goes on to explain: 'In this interpretation I came across four sequences of numbers which revealed the calculations behind the signs. They number 56; this number is significant in that it corresponds to three times the movement of the moon from one end to the other. This number is found in Stonehenge where the astronomically significant stones are surrounded by a circular wall with 56 cavities known as the "Aubrey holes" . . . In the two rows of lines ending in curves at Locmariaquer 29 can be counted pointing to the left and 27 pointing to the right. These numbers too have some relation-

ship with the moon. In round numbers, 29 days are in fact the period which elapses between two similar phases of the moon. This interval of time, the period between two successive full moons, is called a moon lunation or a synodic month. In a space of 27 days the moon returns to the same place in the sky, approximately back to the same star (a sidereal month). This study of the numbers led me to the conclusion that the supporting stone of the grave must have been a lunar calendar. This idea receives further confirmation if the small semi-circles on the left side are counted. There are 19. This is also a significant number as the moon takes 19 years to go from one end to the other.'

Is Müller right in his assumptions, or is he merely pointing out coincidences? Who can say? But even if the engravings on the 'Table des Marchands' do have some astronomical significance, what do the decorations of a completely different kind in the British Isles mean? and what have they to do with the engravings which cover the stones of the burial mound at Gavrinis near Larmor-Plage in south Brittany?

145 to 147   The stones of the many megalithic graves in France are also heavily decorated, as can be seen from these pictures.
145 (above left) Supporting stone from the 'Table des Marchands' near Carnac, covered with engraved lines ending in curves.

146 (above right) 147 (next page)   Elaborate decorations on the walls of the burial chambers of Gavrinis in the south of Brittany.

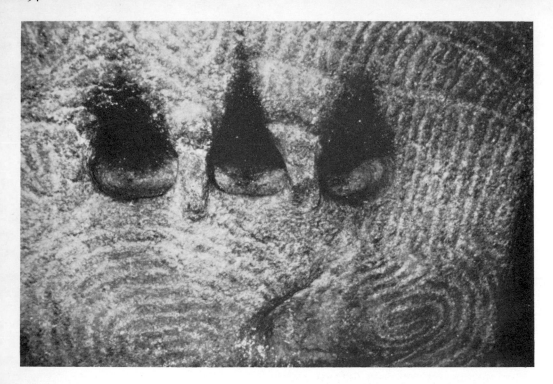

How does it come about that many decorative patterns, as for example the unending double spiral from Scotland, are found in nearly the same form in the east of Ireland 500 km away and also in the Canary Islands? (See ill. 139, 140; 204 and 205 on pages 189, 256 and 257.) Is there any truth in the speculations which suggest that the reason for these patterns being diffused over such great distances was that our ancestors carried them as tattoo markings on their bodies – like the decorations with which native tribes, living at the cultural level of people of the Stone Age, cover themselves?

The questions are endless. The engravings on the megaliths have not yet revealed their true meaning. Will we be able to unravel their secrets or will the ancient graves remain for ever an unsolved mystery?

Fertility Stones and Burial Ships

'By their deeds ye shall know them' is a useful maxim when there is an occasion to judge human strength, perseverance and spiritual greatness. But it is not a magic formula which can be used to reveal the characters of 'doers of deeds' as people, burdened as they are with all their dreams, hopes and fears. When great deeds speak so convincingly as in the case of the megalithic monuments, the prehistorian easily succumbs to the temptation to have only one point of view. There is no doubt that the people who erected the megalithic monuments did in fact move huge boulders of rock for dozens of kilometres; they did make stones which were as tall as houses stand upright; they did raise them as horizontal roofing slabs; they did handle the massive building materials in their geometrically built structures with a precision which was comparable to the accuracy of a theodolite; and they did align their buildings exactly according to the movement of the constellations. But that was not all that they lived for. They did not spend all their days putting up stones and continuously correcting their positions so that they pointed exactly to the full moon as it sets. No man would have regarded this as his sole life's purpose.

Anyone who wants to judge the builders of the megalithic structures exclusively by their feats in building barrows will of necessity have a very one-sided picture of them. The mistake begins with talk about *one* megalithic culture. This concept is valid in the sense that the megalithic idea united the peoples of ancient Europe in a common outlook but it would be wrong to deduce from this unified culture that there was one single unified people in Europe. The people who believed in the megalithic idea were of very different ethnic origins, just as nowadays the builders of skyscrapers can equally well be Americans, Frenchmen, Germans, Russians or Africans.

In the Europe of the megalithic period, differences show up wherever the unifying influence of the architecture or the common ritual did not predominate, but where the dominant note was set by deep individual human feelings, by the wishes and aspirations peculiar to a people or by hopes and anxieties. Such feelings cannot be expressed in megalithic yards, nor can they be calculated on the computers of modern archaeologists. They leave behind hardly any concrete traces. Examples of these are to be found in the remains of bones and traces of fires which archaeologists sometimes discovered within the old stone circles. These have led to theories about places of sacrifice, or sanctuaries where human beings wanted to be near their god or their gods in order to thank them or to ask them for something or to repent. But these are assumptions of a very general nature.

We owe our small increase in knowledge of the customs, the life and death of ancient Europeans, to two sources of information: firstly, ancient folklore which has been passed down through an amazingly long chain of generations to the present century; secondly, as far as the Bronze and Iron Ages are concerned, the accounts of Greek, Roman, and Arabian eyewitnesses telling of contemporary, isolated cultures which even then had a long history behind them.

For example, there are the peculiar holestones in the British Isles about whose meaning we would have known nothing, had they not had a significance for the local population until a few decades ago. The local farmers say that the 'Mên-an-Tol' or 'Crickstone' near Morvah in Cornwall (see ill. 148), can cure children suffering from rickets if they crawl through its hole. According to tradition the stone attracts terrestrial currents which meet at a focal point in the middle of the hole.

148 The 'Mên-en-Tol' or 'Cruckstone' near Morvah in Cornwall, according to popular tradition, has possessed magic powers for thousands of years . . .

The holestone of Doagh in County Antrim in Northern Ireland (see ill. 149), is also reputed to be endowed with secret powers. Young couples who, after their betrothal, touch hands through the hole in the stone can strengthen their union by this contact and should be able to look forward to a happy marriage and healthy children. These popular customs give expression to the desire for health and the hope of fertility. The Mousa Broch, in the Shetland Islands, which is one of the 700 prehistoric inhabited towers to be found in Scotland, could actually be an illustration of one of the basic principles of the British way of life, 'a man's home is his castle' (see ill. 150 and 151). Most of these private fortified dwellings, which are nearly all situated in the middle of fertile arable land near

149   . . . similar powers were attributed the holestone of Doagh`in County Antrim in Northern Ireland.

150   There are still a number of unanswered questions about the purpose of the Brochs, the prehistoric towers found in Scotland such as the one on Mousa, in the Shetland Islands. Some believe they may have been dwellings.

the coast, date from the Bronze and Iron Ages. Some go back to the New Stone Age, to the period of the megaliths. Dwelling places like Mousa Broch reflect the ordinary man's desire for safety and security within his own four walls, and again it is the spoken word which seems to confirm the ancient inhabitants of Scotland's attitude to life.

In addition to the 'brochs' in Scotland there are also prehistoric 'weems'. These are large underground rooms devoid of any light which reflect the desire for a shelter in darkness and seclusion. Weem and the old Scottish word wamha signify related ideas. Wamha means hollow, and wame describes a particular kind of hollow, the womb, to use a modern English word. Here is the common linguistic origin which, in the tradition of the spoken word, perhaps gives an indication of the connections between the security afforded by the mother's body to the embryo and the security afforded by these cave-like dwelling places of prehistoric times. There is no evidence to prove this. It is hardly more than a bold speculation but it is an example of one of many possible interpretations. It is impossible to give precise proof of human feelings, but only more or less credible indications. It is, however, sometimes worth while mentioning this sort of random thought, in case one day further evidence is forthcoming which could turn a possibility into a probability.

One of the turning points of archaeology occurs when, on a site of human activity which has been abandoned for thousands of years, it succeeds in re-creating a picture of colourful and pulsating life. A windfall of this kind has occurred in northern Europe.

In Denmark and southern Scandinavia examples of a later development of megalithic graves can be found in the hundreds of so-called ship burials. These consist of graves made of large stones laid out in the form of ships. The oldest of these go back far into the Bronze Age, and have direct links with megalithic culture. Later, towards the end of prehistoric times, the Vikings interred their dead who were usually cremated in real ships which they buried in mounds of earth. If it is true that most of the external forms of a tradition have been preserved for more than twenty centuries, then it is reasonable to assume the same of the social activities of people who buried their dead so unusually. On this point old Viking legends have been sustained, according to which after the battle of Bråvalla Odin took the dead in a golden ship to Walhalla in the south. This is the reason that nearly all Nordic ship burials took place with the bow of the ship pointing upright to the mid-day sun.

151 (opposite)   The interior of the Mousa Broch is cool and almost devoid of light.

152   A ship burial near Glavendrup on the Danish island of Fyn. In southern Scandinavia these so-called ship burials superseded the Megalithic graves.

153   The elongated oval pattern in which the stones are laid out is characteristic of ship burials, as shown in the one near Lejre on the island of Sjaelland in Denmark.

But there is an even more vivid description, which has all the colour and liveliness of an eye-witness's account of everything that went on at a ship burial. This comes from the 'Risâla', the travelogue of the Arabian merchant Ibn Fadlân, whom the Caliph of Baghdad had sent with other merchants to the Nordic settlements on the Volga in the years 921 and 922 A.D. There to his fascination he witnessed one of the last traditional ceremonial burial rites of a Viking chieftain. This is the account given by Ibn Fadlân:

'I saw Russians (by "Russians" Fadlân meant the Vikings) who had settled on the Volga after first coming as traders. Never have I seen human beings with more perfectly built bodies. They are as tall as date-palm trees. Each of them carries an axe, a sword, and a knife which they never sharpen. The women wear necklaces of gold and silver. The story is told that when a chieftain dies, his death is followed by a number of ceremonies of which the burning of the corpse is the least remarkable. For this reason I was anxious to learn the truth, and one day I heard that one of their distinguished men had died. They laid him in a grave and covered him for ten days until his robes were completed. When it was a rich man who had died they collected his fortune and divided it into three parts, one of which went to his family, another of which was spent on his robes, and the third was devoted to supplying the "nabid" (beer?) which was drunk on the day when his slave girl killed herself and was burned with her master. When a chieftain died his family said to his slave girls and servants, "Who of you is ready to die?" When one of them answered that he was, there was no going back on his word.

'In this case a slave girl came forward and two other slave girls were ordered to watch over her and to follow her wherever she went and to wash her hands and feet. The slave girl drank and sang with joy that heralded her forthcoming good fortune.

'As the day approached when the dead man was to be burned with his slave girl I went to the river where his ship was lying. It had been drawn up onto the land and placed on a wooden support. The people began to move about talking all the time. While the dead man was still lying in his grave they put a bench on the ship and covered it with cloths and cushions and silks painted in the Byzantine style. Then there came an old woman, called the angel of death, who spread the covers over the bench. She was in charge of preparing the death robes and also of killing the slave girl. She was very tall, fat, and forbidding. As she approached the grave they removed the earth and the wooden cover and took off the clothes in which he had died. He had turned black from the cold of the earth where he had lain with the "nabid", fruits, and a stringed musical instrument. They then dressed him in trousers, boots, jacket, and a coat of painted silk with golden buttons, and put on his head a cap of silk and sable skin. After this they took him into the tent, which had been brought out onto the boat, and seated him, supported by cushions, on the carpet. Bread, meat and onions were thrown in front of him. A dog was cut into two and thrown into the ship. All his weapons were laid out beside him. Two horses were allowed to gallop until they broke out into a sweat. They were then cut with a sword into pieces, which were thrown onto the ship. The same happened with two cows. After this a cock and a hen were killed and thrown onto the ship. The slave girl who had expressed the wish to die went from one tent to another and had intercourse with the lord of the tent who said, "Tell your master that I have done this out of love for you." On the Friday afternoon she was raised three times by the men over a temporary structure resembling a door frame which they had erected. The first time she said, "Look! I see my father and my mother"; the second time, "Look! I see all my dead relatives"; the third time, "Look! I see my master sitting in Paradise and Paradise is lovely and green and next to him are men and young boys. He is calling to me. Let me go to him!" Then she was led to the ship where she took off two ankle rings and gave them to the angel of death, who led her onto the ship. But as the girl was not yet allowed to go into the tent, she was offered a cup of "nabid" over which she sang and then drank, taking leave of her friends. Then the girl was given another cup over which she sang for a long time till the old woman pressed her to drink and to go to her master in the tent. At this point she became confused, but the old woman led her into the tent. This was the sign for the men to beat on their shields so that her cries would not be heard. Six men then went into the tent and had intercourse with her and laid her next to her dead master. Two of the men held her legs and two her hands while the angel of death put a strap round her neck and gave the ends to two men whose task it would be to pull them tight. Then the angel of death stepped forward and plunged a dagger with a broad blade into the ribs of the girl while the men strangled her with the strap.

'This was the sign for a man who was the nearest relative of the dead man to step forward and set fire to a piece of wood. Completely naked he walked backwards to the ship. His face was turned towards the people, holding the piece of wood in one hand, the other being placed behind his back. He then set fire to the wooden support which had been put under the ship. Thereupon everybody came forward with a piece of burning wood and threw it onto the funeral pyre which went up in a mighty and fearsome blaze.

'It took less than an hour for the ship, the wood, the slave girl and the chieftain to be reduced to ashes. Then on the place where the ship had stood after it had been pulled out of the river, the people erected what looked like a circular mound. In the middle of this they put up a pole of birch wood and wrote on it the name of the man and his king.'

What happened in Corsica 32 Centuries Ago

The account taken from the traveller's diary of Ibn Fadlân makes realistic, but gruesome, reading. But horror has many faces. One of the old tales from Corsica has all the uncanniness of a fairy-tale. The legend still lives on amongst the inhabitants and anyone who is fortunate enough to be there should listen when on a winter's evening one of the old men, wrinkled by the wind and weather of his native island, tells his tale with all the seriousness that it deserves, but nevertheless playfully winking from time to time:

'The event about which I want to talk occurred in ancient times and there is no longer anyone alive who was present when this strange story occurred. But it is true, my father told it to me when I was still a small boy.

'As everyone knows, there were once vampires on our island; they were dead men who rose by night out of their graves and lay in wait for young girls or even on occasion attacked them in their rooms. Whenever they found a young victim they buried their long pointed eye teeth deep into their necks or breasts and drank eagerly from the blood which spouted forth. Once upon a time a vampire lived near our village and naturally the men and women of the parish tried to render the monster harmless as quickly as possible. But that was not so simple. For by day the horrible bloodsucker lay peacefully in his grave, and in the darkness of the nights on which he sought out his victims it was only too easy for him to escape. The crafty inhabitants of our village decided therefore to set a trap for him. They knew that he liked to perform his monstrous deeds in the dimly lit woods near the old stone chapel which lies some distance from the vicarage. So they decided to send a particularly pretty and attractive young girl there who, despite her gentle manner and her marriageable age, was still pure and a virgin. For everyone knows that vampires are specially fond of such maidens to satisfy their thirst for blood. If the beautiful child could manage to charm the resurrected dead man then it should be easy to overpower and impale him. For this, as is generally known, is the only way to finish off a vampire for all time.

'But everything turned out differently from the way the good people had planned. The young girl went by night to the lonely place and the villagers followed behind her armed with sticks and stakes. But as the slim form of the girl reached the church door there was no trace of the vampire. However, inside the church the faltering steps of the girl were heard by a young man who, by mishap, had been locked into the church after the service. He was thinking that he would have to stay in his prison the whole week and feared that perhaps he might even die of hunger or thirst. Suddenly he heard someone was moving outside. It was just at this very moment that the young girl fearfully called out to the vampire. The young man, seeing his rescue at hand, answered with a loud cry which reverberated against the bare stone walls of the church in a hollow and ghostlike fashion. The young girl outside was rooted to the ground and her heart stopped beating with stark terror. She grew stiff and was immediately turned into stone.

'This all happened before time immemorial but the stone fashioned in human shape, still stands next to the old church of Santa Maria. The doors and windows of the church are nailed up and are a reminder of the terrifying night when the inhabitants of our village hoped to entice a vampire into a trap.'

The human-shaped stone next to the church of Santa Maria really does exist (see ill. 2 on page 10). But the legend which surrounds it is one of fantasy, without the solid core of truth which legends handed down by word of mouth sometimes do have. Furthermore, the remarkable statue happens to be much older than the little Romanesque church. The difference in age between them is nearly two thousand years. However, the legend has actually achieved one thing; it has been the source of all the speculation surrounding the unsolved mystery of the stone figure since the beginning of history. It is, moreover, but one of three quite different stories which are told about the same stone and which were tracked down by the French archaeologist Roger Grosjean and his colleagues. What is the real basis of this, and some dozens of similar stone columns on the wild and mountainous Mediterranean island, was a curious enigma for a long time. Exactly two decades ago, with the discovery of the human shaped menhir statues of Filitosa, the first light began to penetrate the veil which till then had lain over Corsican prehistory. In the meantime further finds had produced new scraps of knowledge, but on this island, rich in legends, each riddle which is solved seems to produce a bigger one from the shadows of the past. That was the situation before the discovery of Filitosa in 1956. As Roger Grosjean has written: 'For 150 years there appears to have been a spell cast over investigations into prehistoric times in Corsica. In the 160 works which have been written on that subject there can be found no passage which would fit into any other. On the contrary they are full of statements which are at variance with the truth such as: "There are very few megalithic monuments in Corsica."'

In fact Corsica is specially rich in stone testimonials from megalithic times. As is the case nearly everywhere on the coasts of Europe and North Africa, it began about 3000 B.C. with dolmen and quite ordinary menhirs (see ill. 91 and 92).

154   The paladin near Serra di Ferru is one of the earliest human shaped menhirs on Corsica. It stands 2.91 metres high and weighs 1.5 tons.

Then some thousand years later the Corsican menhirs slowly began to change. The usual stone columns turned into hewn images, narrower at the bottom and broader at the top, flat in front and rounded behind as if they were stylized human bodies without heads or limbs, with broad angular shoulders, flat chests and stomachs and arched backs. Later developments confirm the theory. About 1500 B.C. heads began to appear on the stone shoulders beginning as unhewn spheres, ovals, or cylinders. A little later small recesses began to appear in the faces as mouths and eyes, the chin was clearly marked (see ill. 154). Finally there was added the definite and sometimes even bulbous shape of a nose. The builders of the Corsican megalithic structures had made the first western European monumental statues, many centuries before the crude sculptures of the archaic period in ancient Greece.

Then something strange occurred. From about 1200 B.C. the menhir statues bore arms. Daggers, sabres, and long swords hung diagonally across their stone chests (see ill. 156). Coats of mail protected their chests and backs. Round helmets with upturned edges and distinct neck protectors covered their heads. Obviously, once upon a time horns of bulls must have been fitted to these helmets, because the holes into which these distinctive martial decorations had been inserted can clearly be seen.

155 The stone figures of Filitosa in south Corsica stand out against the shimmering haze of the March skies like phantoms from another world.

156   Sometime about 1200 B.C. the menhir statues in south Corsica began to show weapons. This statue near Filitosa, which is 2.96 metres tall, is carrying a dagger.

This is all very unusual since those who made the menhirs had for thousands of years been a peace-loving people who practised agriculture and stock farming. The fact that they suddenly began to portray warriors in their statues must have meant that they had been attacked. Since Corsica is an island, the enemy must have come by sea. And, in fact, there is further evidence of a military invasion to be found in the south of the island, starting from the bay of Porto-Vecchio. The invaders overturned the old menhir statues and destroyed or buried the stone figures. They destroyed the settlements of the native megalithic people and built fortified towers on the ruins. Near Filitosa in the south-west of the island and near Cucuruzzu, high up in the mountainous country in the south, they built regular castles (see ill. 157 and 158).

Who were these warriors who came over the sea? Prehistorians call them Torriers after the remarkable stone

157 and 158   Around 1200 B.C. mysterious seafarers invaded Corsica and built fortified places such as the castle of Cucuruzzu.

159 Many Corsican menhirs did not survive the centuries upright. Some of them were dismantled by the seagoing invaders. Many were later used by inhabitants of the island as handy building materials. Behind the menhir of Sagone there is a Romanesque church which dates from the 12th century. A human-shaped menhir forms one of its corner-stones, as can be seen in the middle of the right-hand side of the picture.

towers which they built. But that does not tell us anything about who they were or from where they came. The menhir statues of armed men can help here. The old native population of Corsica were still living in the Stone Age at the time of the attack. They had no knowledge of either bronze or iron. Their weapons were spears with heads made of stone. But when the sculptors of those days suddenly began to make statues of warriors with metal daggers, sabres and swords, they could not have been portraying their own people. They were representing the enemy. Why they did this, has been the subject of controversy. Perhaps to commemorate the heroic actions of their dead by placing statues of the conquered enemy round the graves of their own warriors as was once the custom in southern Siberia.

160   In north Corsica, unarmed menhir statues were still being erected by the indigenous population which had fled there in the face of invasion. Many of these statues, like this menhir not far from Tavera, possess an archaic beauty which is very rare.

In any case the mysterious invaders must have carried the same weapons as the menhirs of that period. Like these they must have worn on their chests and backs, metal coats of mail with five deep grooves, and they must have used a round helmet with a neck-shield and bull's horns on top to protect their heads. A bas-relief on a wall of the Temple of Medinet-Habu, 3,000 kilometres away in Egypt (see ill. 161), portrays warriors who looked exactly like that. The scene represents a naval battle which took place in 1190 B.C. between the mysterious aggressors and the Egyptian fleet. At that time warring hordes of the same race were infesting large stretches of the Mediterranean. It could only have been they, the so-called 'Torriers', who attacked Corsica at that time. Archaeologists gave the name 'sea people' to those marauding sailors who made the Mediterranean unsafe some 32 centuries ago. They even make a distinction between different groups, the Shardana, for example, or the Philistines. But this still does not say anything about who these people really were and from where they came. They could not have come from the Mediterranean area because no people, however warlike it

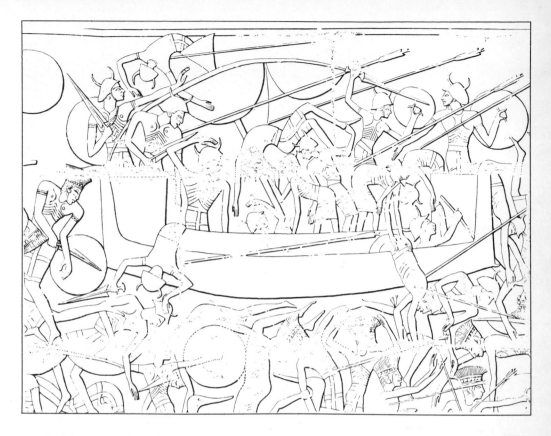

161 The bas-relief from the Egyptian temple of Medinet-Habu depicts a battle between the sea peoples and the Egyptians. The deeply grooved metal coats of mail, the round shields, and the horned helmets, are all typical of the warrior sea rovers.

may be, devastates its own country. This is why the theories of many historians that the sea people came from Palestine, the Aegean islands, Crete, Greece, Thessaly or Macedonia are certainly incorrect. In fact they attacked and destroyed all these regions around 1200 B.C. But where, then, was the native land of these mysterious hordes?

Legendary Atlantis – the Home of the Sea People

The large bas-relief from the Egyptian Temple of Medinet-Habu clearly illustrates the unusual equipment of the sea-faring warriors which was certainly not in every-day use: their long swords with characteristic handles, their helmets decorated with horns or plumes, their typical round shields and their ships with bows and sterns that tapered off like the long neck of a swan, and ended with a stylized carving of a bird's head. These vividly recall the ships in the rock carvings in southern parts of Scandinavia (see ill. 89 p. 144). Is the resemblance a coincidence?

In the National Museum of Copenhagen there are swords dating from the Nordic Bronze Age whose shape amazingly resembles the pointed weapons of the sea peoples. In the

162   The small bronze figure found in the Nuraghe at Abini in Sardinia portrays a seafaring warrior with two round shields and a horned helmet . . .

Museum there is also a bronze comb, the handle of which is worked into the shape of a halo or plumed crown. The apparent coincidences are so numerous as to suggest a possible link between north and south.

On Sardinia, the island close to Corsica, small bronze statuettes representing armed warriors have been found in the nuraghi, the tower-shaped constructions which are peculiar to the island (see ill. 162). Their round shields, the characteristic sword handles and the horned helmets clearly indicate that they belonged to the sea peoples. The horns which decorate their helmets are especially long and end in round knobs. Archaeologists found an almost exact replica of the horn-shaped helmet on the island of Sjaelland in Denmark.

Does this mean that hordes set out from southern Scandinavia and Denmark around 1200 B.C. to conquer the Mediterranean region? An inscription in the Temple of

163 Archaeologists found an identical helmet in Denmark.

Medinet-Habu reads as follows: 'No country could resist them. Hatti (the kingdom of the Hittites), Kode (a region in Asia Minor), Carchemish (on the Euphrates), Yereth (in Crete?) and Yeres (in Cyprus) were all destroyed in one campaign. They pitched their camp in the land of the Amorites (an Egyptian province) and laid the land to waste, and wiped out the people as if they had never existed. Wherever they arrived a flame beckoned them and they reached out towards the sea, their hearts filled with confidence. "Our plans will succeed," they said.'

They could not have been few in number. If it is true that northern European people advanced on the Mediterranean, they could not have done so by sending out small expeditionary forces. They must surely have emigrated from their ancient native land in large numbers. It is true that there have been hardly any archaeological finds on the Danish islands or on the Scandinavian mainland which date from the period after the middle of the 13th century B.C. The ancient inhabitants had left these lands. But what had been the reason for their sudden flight?

In 1911 the climatologist, D. Wildvang, wrote in his book about 'a prehistoric catastrophe on the North Sea coast of Germany': 'With its characteristic unbridled force the North Sea overflowed for the first time to the edge of the Geest river. The high salt content of its waves caused the destruction of all vegetation. At the first impact, luxuriant trees appeared to have crashed to the ground . . . Everywhere the tops of the fallen trees pointed to the east, which seemed to confirm the supposition that the catastrophe was caused by a storm coming from a westerly direction.' Wildvang based his theories on the results of innumerable drilling experiments carried out in the course of cutting of peat and the building of canals and sluices in northern Germany. The terrible catastrophe must have taken place towards the end of the second millenium before Christ, at a time when many of the great European volcanoes had erupted simultaneously. In the Aegean Sea, the Santorini eruption ejected red-hot stone and hot ashes over an area of more than 130 cubic kilometres; Etna became active, and very probably huge streams of lava poured from the volcanoes of Sinai and Iceland into the sea. Sea tremors transformed the waves into swiftly moving walls of surf as high as houses and drove them onto the mainland, devastating large tracts of land. Fire-spewing mountains threw unimaginable quantities of extremely fine ash high into the atmosphere and obscured the light of the sun. A drastic fall in temperature followed. In historic times severe volcanic eruptions have had similar effects on the climate. For example, after the great eruption of the Krakatoa in the year 1883 the average annual temperature in the whole world fell by 0.5°C, and in many lands the harvest failed. The cool summers and the extreme cold winters of the years 1784 and 1786 were preceded by a major volcanic eruption: Skaptarjökull in Iceland became active on 11th June 1783.

The devastating catastrophe which fell with particular force on the countries bordering on the North Sea seems to have been responsible for its old Celtic name of Marimarusa, and its designation by the Greeks as the *thalassa nekron* and *nekros pontos*. These all mean *the sea of the dead* and the Romans also gave the same designation to the North Sea, calling it *mare mortuum*. There is no doubt that the unleashing of the natural forces and the subsequent marked deterioration of the climate and the permanent flooding of large stretches of land west of the present-day Jutland and Schleswig-Holstein were sufficient reasons for the ancient northern peoples to leave their devastated land and to seek a new home. This might explain the sudden appearance of the vast armies of the sea peoples in the Mediterranean regions around the year 1220 B.C., and the amazing resemblance of their arms, head-dress and ships to those of the north European people.

Does this connection also throw light on the true background of the legend of Atlantis, which has been the subject of so much discussion and of so much fierce controversy in the professional world? At the beginning of the 3rd century B.C. the Greek philosopher and writer Plato describes in some 20 pages the report of his uncle Critias. Plato lets Critias tell what he had learned when he was nine years old from his 90-year-old grandfather. The grandfather, it is said, had in turn heard the story from his father, Dropides, who had learned it from his friend Solon about 600 B.C. Solon referred to the archives of Egyptian priests from which he had obtained his knowledge of the tale. This in a few words is the story of the Atlantis legend. Its content can be described equally briefly:

Beyond the pillars of Hercules, that is to say, beyond the Rock of Gibraltar there was once a mighty empire. It was a union of ten kingdoms, the centre of which was said to be a small island, Basileia, in the 'atlantic sea'. In addition the rulers of this empire held sway over many other islands, part of the mainland and also areas in the Mediterranean region, in North Africa as far as Egypt and in Europe as far as Italy.

According to the Atlantis legend, the Egyptian priests told Solon that: 'This union with its concentrated power made the attempt to subjugate your land and our land and the whole Mediterranean region in one single campaign. In this situation, O Solon, through its bravery and skill the army of your native Athens distinguished itself before all mankind. Athens, which surpassed all others in courage and military prowess – first at the head of all Greeks and then left to fight on its own – was extremely hard pressed but finally overcame the aggressor and stopped him from subjugating those who had not yet fallen under his yoke and helped us others to achieve freedom. At a later date powerful earthquakes and floods took place and your Greek army vanished from the earth in the course of one terrible day and one night. In the same way the island of Atlantis sank into the sea and vanished from eyesight. As a result a coat of slimy substance was left on the surface of the sea by the sunken island, the sea even to this day is no longer navigable or accessible to scientific examination.'

The legend also tells of sacrificial rites and bull-fights, of the meeting of kings and drafting laws in ancient Atlantis, and praises the skill of the citizens in sport, in battle and at sea. When the Egyptian priests told Solon about Atlantis they said that the kingdom had sunk into the sea 8,000 or 9,000 years previously. Whatever truth the legend may have – and Plato emphasized the truth of his report quite explicitly on a number of occasions – the time factor could not possibly have been correct. The citizens of Atlantis, according to Plato's report, used utensils and weapons made of iron, which metal only came into use 2,000 years B.C. The anachronism was first spotted by Olaf Rudbeck, the Rector of the University of Uppsala, around the year 1700. His explanation was that Plato, when he talked of 8,000 years, must have been talking of 8,000 months, because in Solon's time the Egyptians used a calendar which was calculated in months. The story told about Atlantis would then have taken place towards the middle of the 13th century B.C. This suddenly gave a lead for a possible explanation. Jürgen Spanuth, a parson in north Germany as well as a prehistorian and archaeologist, was the first to express this view in 1953 in his controversial book *The Solution to the Mystery of Atlantis*. He identified the sea peoples with the citizens of the Atlantis of Plato's legend and looked for Basileia, the royal island of the sunken empire, to the east of Helgoland. In the meantime in the shallow waters of the 'Steingrund' (stony bottom) divers actually found ruins of walls shaped by human hands (see ill. 164).

164   In the shallow waters of the 'Steingrund' (stony bottom), east of Helgoland, divers found ruins of man made flintstone walls. Bronze Age inhabitants of Denmark obtained the materials from mines which exist to this day such as the prehistoric flint mine at Hou.

Spanuth supported his theory of Atlantis with an impressive mass of evidence consisting of the identity of the warlike
sea peoples with the ancient inhabitants of the nordic regions;
the remarkable similarity between Plato's report and the
remains of a Bronze Age civilization which had been found in
south Scandinavia and Denmark; and also the amazing
parallel between the overwhelming national catastrophe
referred to in the legend and the terrible devastation which
actually occurred in northern Europe around 1220 B.C.

Spanuth's work received spontaneous recognition in the
professional world. Professor P. Paulsen wrote in a mem-
orandum dated 1.6.1949: 'After thorough examination of the
scientific work of Pastor J. Spanuth and after reading the
manuscript of a book about *The Solution to the Mystery of
Atlantis*, I hereby declare that they deal with very significant
and valuable research which should in every way be supported.' And Professor Otto Huth wrote to the author when
his book appeared in 1953 saying: 'I read your book right
through in one night and congratulate you on this magnificent
presentation of your thesis and on your discovery.'

But the professional world was soon up in arms and
attacked the Pastor in no uncertain manner, calling him a liar
and retailer of 'invented nonsense', but without being able to
contradict him. Public opinion took the side of the professors
who were the most vociferous in attacking Spanuth. In the
end the Pastor, who was driven into a corner, took his
opponents to court. On 2.12.1960 the *Frankfurter Rundschau*
commented as follows on the judgement of the court: 'After
an action in the Landgericht of Flensburg, the ten professors
withdrew their plea because they admitted that their arguments against Spanuth were untenable, which it must be
admitted was not an every-day occurrence in the realm of
German science.' It was by no means true that Spanuth had
only found opponents. Some six years before the judgement
of the court of Flensburg, Professor Stokar, the well-known
prehistorian, in a letter to his colleague Jacob-Friesen spoke
out against an anti-Spanuth brochure which had been
published by the ten professors who later appeared before the
court: 'This brochure is not a well reasoned piece of work but
a disgrace! These are not scientific, well documented arguments, but the cluckings of frightened hens of a very low
standard. I am appalled. The pamphlet *The Solution to the
Mystery of Atlantis* by Weyl refutes everything which has
been discovered in the last 20 years.' Other scientists argued
in much the same way as Professor Stokar.

In spite of everything the scientists' quarrel about

Spanuth's discoveries continues to this day. But independent of whether the mysterious sea peoples were or were not the inhabitants of Plato's Atlantis, there is one thing which in the long run can scarcely be denied: that they came from the far north.

The Nuraghi of Sardinia –
Fortresses, Graves or Sun Temples?

Sardinia, 26th November 1970. A strong autumn wind blew over the arid plains of the lower part of the island near the small village of Trempu. Apart from a few storm clouds the sky was clear but the air cool. There was a piercing wind.

Armed with a compass, tape-measure and a pad of drawing paper, two men, one young and the other middle-aged, set out on foot from the remote village. They followed the main road for some 200 metres to the south and then turned right onto a cart track. As everywhere on the island, the dusty track was bordered by low walls made of stones loosely laid on top of each other. They were surrounded by dry, thorny hedges. In a quarter of an hour the two men had reached their goal: a round structure, four metres high and 12.5 metres in diameter. The style of the ruin showed that the building must be very old. The huge, roughly hewn stones lay on top of each other without any mortar, the outer walls were rough hewn. Two entrances led into the remains of the round building, one exactly on the south side, the other roughly to the north-east.

The two men set about measuring the structure. With the certain touch of people who know their business they quickly drew a ground plan and filled in the measurements, took the bearings of the passages with a compass, and made a sketch of the outside and a cross-section.

Professor Lello Fadda and his assistant had been measuring the nuraghi of Canchedda, one of the 7,000 more or less well-preserved prehistoric towers which in this form exist only on Sardinia (see ill. 165 to 171). At an earlier date there must have been many more of them.

Professor Fadda was a collaborator of Professor Carlo Maxia, who had made it his aim to solve the mystery of the ancient Sardinian towers. At different periods of history scientists before his time had attempted to find answers to the many unsolved questions about the nuraghi. They had speculated on the identity of the builders of these huge towers, and had put forward theories which attempted to explain the original purpose of these vast mysterious buildings. They had tried to determine in which period the nuraghi had been built. The answers were as different and diverse as

165 In recent years, under the direction of Professor Maxias of the University of Cagliari, the study of the Nuraghi of Sardinia has received fresh impetus. Detailed plans, like this one by Professor Fadda, are typical of the intensive research now being done.

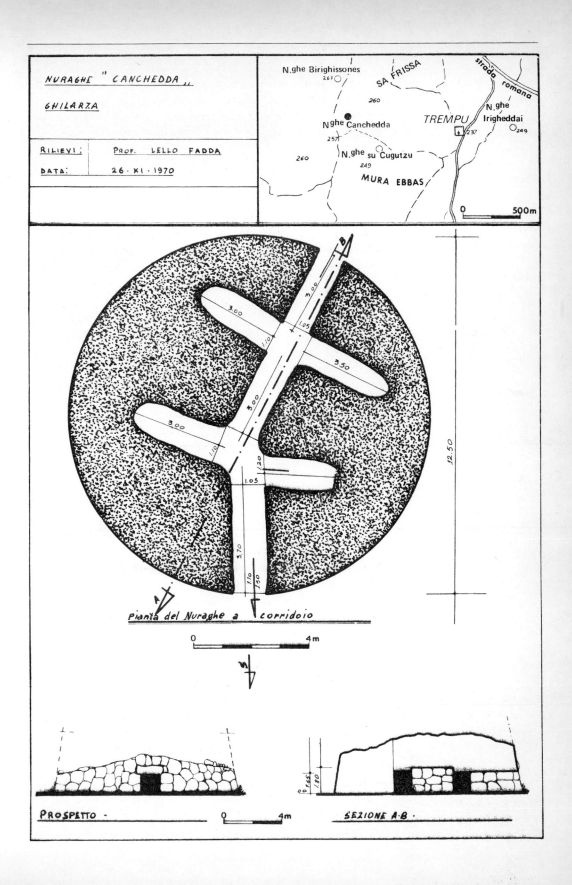

NURAGHE "CANCHEDDA"

GHILARZA

RILIEVI:	PROF. LELLO FADDA
DATA:	26·XI·1970

N.ghe Birighissones
267
SA FRISSA
strada romana
260
N.ghe Canchedda
TREMPU 237
N.ghe Irigheddai
257
249
N.ghe su Cugutzu
260
249
MURA EBBAS

0   500m

Pianta del Nuraghe a corridoio

0   4m

Prospetto -   0   4m   SEZIONE A·B·

166 to 171   The Nuraghi of Sardinia: huge towers assembled of massive stones without mortar or concrete more than 3,000 years ago. The opinions of scientists on their significance vary greatly.

The first results of astro-archaeological investigations favour the theory that they were solar temples: 166 (above left)   The Nuraghe of S'Oro in the mountainous country 10 kms south of Muravera in the south-east of Sardinia.

*167 and 168 (opposite, above right and below)   The Nuraghe of Santa Barbara near Macomer,
169 (above) and 170 (below, left)   The Nuraghe of Losa near Abbasanta, 171   The Nuraghe of
Santa Antine near Torralba.*

the number of scientists who expressed them. They began with no less a person than Aristotle who in the fourth century B.C. referred to Jolaus, the son of Ificles, as the builder of the nuraghi, in his treatise *De mirabilibus auscultationibus*.

The Greek author Timaeus in about 300 B.C. attributed the construction of the massive towers to Daedalus, the first craftsman, according to the legend of his people. Daedalus was also reported to have been responsible for building, on the orders of Minos, the King of Crete, the world-famous subterranean labyrinth for Minotaur, the wild bull.

Later scientists believed that Spanish grandees who had emigrated from the mainland were the architects of the nuraghi. Others believed that immigrants from the Orient had built the towers. At different times the Egyptians, Carthaginians, Etruscans, Phoenicians and even the Celts were considered to have been responsible for the massive circular structures. Or could they have simply been the work of native peasants?

Various attempts were made to put a date on the structures, which were as wide apart as 'past the Ice Age' and attributed to the 'Iron Age'.

The supposed uses of the nuraghi are no less varied. Suggestions were made about Egyptian graves as well as residences for ancient inhabitants of gigantic stature, mausoleums for distinguished dead, community centres, temples devoted to mystical fire-rites, victory monuments, fortifications, watch-towers or houses similar to those which were still being built in 18th century France.

For anybody who has carefully studied the nuraghi, it is certain that there is not much to be said for most of these interpretations. There is no question of the nuraghi being buildings for everyday use, whatever their purpose may have been. Their method of construction makes any stay within these cyclopaean walls far from pleasant. Complete darkness reigns in the long window-less corridors and the central corbel vaulted chambers (see ill. 172). There is no trace of any ventilation holes through which the smoke of a domestic fire might escape. And for the greater part of the year it is so damp inside the nuraghi that after a short time any inmate would suffer from rheumatism or arthritis. Moreover, there has never been any excavation which gave any indication that these colossal towers had been used as dwellings, community centres, fortifications or watch-towers. Until now no traces have been found either of kitchen waste or fireplaces.

The theory which is generally accepted in works on prehistory that the nuraghai were fortifications comes up

172 to 174 Dark passages and chambers are typical of the interiors of the Nuraghi. The three illustrations (opposite and on the following page) are of the impressive structure of the Nuraghe at Sant' Antine.

against another argument. Originally there must have been more than 12,000 nuraghi on Sardinia. It is impossible to accept that there should have been 12,000 fortifications in such a small area, especially since, according to the supporters of this theory, each fortress must have had its own commander. Fortifications do not unite a military force, they divide it into unmanageable and ineffectual groups. Furthermore, the drain on manpower would be so great that it would no longer be possible to satisfy the needs of agriculture. Moreover, whom could such a martial people attack, seeing that they were the only inhabitants of the island, or against whom should this military might defend the fatherland which had never been attacked for more than 1,000 years?

The only possible conclusion to be drawn is, therefore, that the nuraghi must have been burial places or temples. If they were burial places the question immediately arises, how did the inhabitants bury their dead before they built the nuraghi? The answer is: in the beginning in dolmen graves, which was the case nearly everywhere on the coastlines of Europe, and later in the 'tombe dei giganti' (the giants' tombs) peculiar to Sardinia which, like the dolmen, date from the megalithic period, and then in the 'domu de janas' which were graves hewn out of the massive rock often with a number of separate

175   *The grave of Sant' Andria Priu, which is hewn out of the cliff, lies to the east of the little town of Bonorva in Sardinia.*

chambers (see ill. 175 to 178). The builders of the nuraghi maintained in their original form, the death rites of the 'domu de janas'. For this reason there is nothing to be said for the theory that the big stone towers might also have been burial chambers.

In any event, Professor Maxia believes that the nuraghi may have been a resting-place for the dead, if only a temporary one. The ancient Sardinians often entombed several dozens of their dead in the graves in the rocks, as has been shown by a number of finds of skeletons. Removed from the direct influence of light, wind, rain and sun in these subterranean chambers, and immune from the attacks of vultures which until the last century were still common in Sardinia, the corpses in the 'domu de janas' would only have decayed very slowly. The unbearable stink would have made further burials impossible for a long time. It is true that the people of the Stone Age also laid their dead to rest in large communal chambers, but they did not bury complete corpses, only the dry bones devoid of flesh. For a few days the corpses were exposed to the weather, bacteria and vultures to become skeletons. They were then laid in specially designated stone circles which are still to be found to this day in Sardinia.

176 (opposite)   The chambers in the interior are carefully carved out of the massive rock.

177   The rays of light from a pocket torch pick out the outline of two graves.

178   On the table mountain above the rock tomb of Sant' Andria Priu there is a dolmen type of stone structure. The ancient inhabitants of Sardinia hewed it out of the living rock.

Could the nuraghi have been temples which served the same purpose as the ancient circles? Were they 'Towers of Silence' like the Dakhma in the Parsee sect founded by Zoroaster! In any case the terraces of the numerous nuraghi would have been ideal as sites for exposing corpses to the wind, weather and carrion vultures and turning them into skeletons. Could the origin of the word nuraghi be traced back to the Phoenician word 'nur-hag', 'tower of fire'? The increase in phosphorus, as a result of the many corpses reduced to skeletons over the years, must have shed a ghostly light on the towers. Professor Maxia considers that it is quite possible that such a macabre connection existed. The Sardinian scientist and his colleagues had carefully taken the measurements of hundreds of nuraghi and today are still examining other structures with compasses and tape-measures. Their main objective, however, is not to prove that their island ancestors used the towers exclusively for turning corpses into skeletons before their actual burial in the rock chambers. That could have been a secondary objective. The main point of the Professor's investigations lay in a different direction. He believed that the nuraghi were sun temples like Stonehenge and he is using the techniques of astro-archaeology to investigate the ancient structures. His anthropological institute has worked out a joint programme of studies with the astronomical institute of the same university. 'The examination of the nuraghi with the technical methods of archaeology,' says Professor Maxia, 'has not only failed to further our knowledge of this civilization, but it has produced a completely false picture. As has been the case with similar examples of Megalithic culture, it is only possible finally to unravel the mysteries of the nuraghi with the techniques of astro-archaeology, which have proved their effectiveness.'

Professor Maxia has been actively engaged in the unravelling of this mystery for a number of years: in 1974 he published the first results of his work in a 56-page manuscript. The entrances of most nuraghi face directly south, and the layout of the internal passages and courtyards was so designed that it was possible to deduce that they were connected with observations of movements of the sun. Some nuraghi were exceptions to this rule. In many cases the entrances appeared to point in the direction of the sunrise at the time of the winter solstice; in others in the direction of the rise of particularly bright stars, for example Rigel in the constellation of Orion, or Sirius.

Another interesting discovery was revealed by Professor Maxia's investigations. There appeared to be a direct link between the building activity of the people connected with the nuraghi and the eclipses of the sun and moon which could have been observed from Sardinia in the period between 1200 and 200 B.C. Whenever there was an eclipse of the sun and moon the ancient Sardinians dedicated a new temple, a nuragh, to the god of the sun or the moon to placate them, for fear that they might leave the heavens for ever. 'Of course these first preliminary results need to be supported by the results of a great number of measurements,' commented Professor Maxia on his own work, 'but after years of long and painstaking work I am already convinced that the basis of the culture of the nuraghi was religious and closely connected with the stars, and that therefore it was essentially an astronomic basis.'

If this discovery was valid for the nuraghi themselves, could it also have been significant for other structures belonging to the same culture?

Could not the subterranean burial chambers, the graves of the giants, the menhirs, the sunstones, and the sacrificial altars found near many of the nuraghi perhaps also have been aligned with some star (see ill. 179)? Professor Maxia wants to pursue this question. It will involve a great deal of work, but it may perhaps be worth while. So far only two altar stones have been measured. They appear to have been directed towards the sunrise at the time of the summer solstice. But it is far too early to draw any final conclusion.

On the other hand, today the astronomic significance of the Sardinian 'well temples' is more certain. They are a particular kind of subterranean structure 70 of which have so far been discovered by archaeologists. More than 30 are in a good state of preservation. They are all built in a similar pattern and they are all situated near a nuraghe. Stone steps lead down half-a-dozen metres under the earth and end at a well surrounded by a circular wall, which is spanned by a high, nearly Gothic-shaped vault. The top of the vault reaches up to the surface of the earth and is often open to the skies (see ill. 180 and 181). The stones, which are some 2,500 years old in many of these temples, today look as though they had just been worked with the most modern stone saws (see ill. 182). In contrast with the sun and star temples of the nuraghi, Professor Maxia sees these remarkable well temples as moon sanctuaries. Working with the astrologer Proverbio he was the first to take careful measurements of the structure of Santa Cristina. As it is in an especially fine state of preservation it is possible to take unusually exact measurements. The results which have already been achieved on this site arouse great expectations

179 (opposite)   In the courtyard of the Nuraghe of Sant' Antine there is an altar-stone with a circle representing the sun. The ancient priests of Sardinia presented their liquid offerings here.

180   This is a cross-section of the well temple of Santa Cristina which lies between Macomer and Abbasanta in Sardinia. At the deepest point, about 6 metres under ground, the crystal-clear water from the holy spring still flows.

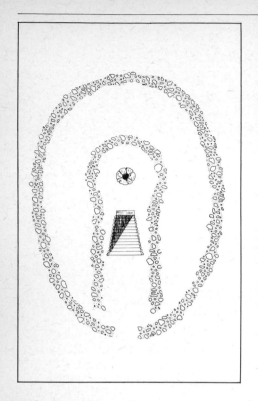

181   This is the plan of the well sanctuary seen from above. Small stone walls surround the steps which lead underground as well as the small hole of the dome at the surface of the earth.

182   The steps to the well temple of Santa Cristina are thousands of years old but could very well have been made only yesterday by modern stonemasons. The carefully cut slabs of stone fit tightly on top of each other without mortar.

for the measurements which are being taken on other well temples. The sacred well of Santa Cristina is laid out with such precision that once a year the full moon casts its light so exactly through the small opening in the top of the vault that shortly after midnight for a few minutes it shines on the water in the well. This annual event occurs at the very moment when an eclipse of the moon can take place! It is of course possible that this is a coincidence, even though a most exceptional one. But the measurements which the two professors took on the equally well-preserved holy well of Santa Vittoria di Serri produced very similar figures. Were the well temples of Sardinia moon observatories? The future alone will show.

Many scientists are sceptical of the work of their zealous Sardinian colleagues. But even if the results of their investigations may one day prove negative, is it not true that Professor Thom in England also began with an assumption which was followed by the first measurements, then by a whole series of calculations and finally by established certainty? The time-consuming and most important work of the team of professors is continuing, and there is no doubt that the discoveries of the two scientists will one day constitute one of the fixed stones in the mosaic of knowledge obtained about the megalithic culture, whatever shape this stone may take in the final analysis.

Talayots, Taulas and Navetas –
Stepchildren of Archaeology

The airport at Frankfurt – the monotonous voice of the loudspeaker in the departure hall for charter planes calls the passengers for the aeroplane to Palma in Mallorca. More than 400 holidaymakers are standing at the exit leading to the gangway to the aircraft, waiting for the stewardess to open the glass door, and push and jostle their way into the jumbo jet in order to secure a good seat. The same scene is repeated almost daily at all the major airports in Europe. Mallorca has become more and more popular over a number of years.

If a single aircraft were to land half-a-dozen archaeologists on the island there would be sufficient work there and on the neighbouring island of Minorca for them, their children and their children's children. But in contrast to their huge success with tourists these islands in the western Mediterranean are not at all popular with archaeologists. Their playgrounds are in the eastern Mediterranean, Crete, Mycenae, Asia Minor and Egypt, where they know what to expect and where they do not risk their reputations, since no new spectacular discovery could be made for which they might not have a satisfactory explanation.

On the Balearic Islands there are dozens of prehistoric villages under the dust of thousands of years. There the ancient stones lie exposed on the surface, and the peasants and road builders use them as the raw materials to build roads and dams, thereby destroying the traces of past civilizations.

Very little more is known about the prehistoric monuments, the countless talayots, the taulas and navetas, peculiar to Mallorca and Minorca than that they exist or did so until recently and that they date from the Bronze Age. On the other hand holidaymakers on Sardinia are aware that there are nuraghi on the island. But how many tourists on Mallorca have seen anything of the 1,000 prehistoric towers which once stood on the island and of which little more than fragments survive? Who knows even one of the many Bronze Age villages, of which so far only two have been superficially and incompletely excavated? (see ill. 183 and 184). Hardly any guide-book mentions them and hardly any map of the island gives the location of more than four or five.

What do the talayots, taulas and navetas look like? Their cyclopean architecture indicates that they were megalithic monuments. The talayots vaguely resemble the nuraghi of Sardinia (see ill. 185 and 186) and were once huge towers standing four or five or more metres high, but today are generally little more than stumps. Many talayots are circular,

183 *The partly excavated prehistoric village of Capicorp Vey is in south-west of Mallorca only a few kilometres north of Vallgornera. The separate dwelling-houses are placed in the outer wall like square cells. On the left background a talayot is set into the wall.*

184 *On the south side of the little town of Artà in eastern Mallorca archaeologists have excavated another prehistoric village called Ses Paisses. The illustration shows one of the triliths in the surrounding wall.*

185 and 186 A small
paved road to the bay of
Estret branches to the north
off the main road between
Artà and Can Picafort. It
runs through flat
pastureland on which there
the two well-preserved
talayots of Santa Canova.
One is round (ill. 185)
and the other is square (ill.
186).

others have a square ground plan. They all have in common a massive central pillar made of heavy unhewn stones, which may have supported the roof of a wood or stone structure (see ill. 187 and 188).

The location of the talayots gives no clue to their original function and these huge structures can be found all over Mallorca, in the arid southern plain as well as in the northern mountains.* The best surviving examples of the mysterious towers are to be found in the Garriga, the arid stony steppe in the south-east, where the soil is barren and parched. In that region there is no agriculture to speak of, and as a result the local peasants have not used the towers as quarries.

* Some of the most beautifully preserved talayots are to be found in the neighbourhood of Lluchmayor, Alcudia, Lloseta, Cala San Vincente, San Jaumell and Artà.

187 and 188 (opposite) The central pillars made of large unhewn circular stones found in every talayot have mystified archaeologists. Did they support a wooden roof? The two illustrations are of the round talayot of Santa Canova.

There are instances of single talayots standing alone in the landscape. Then there are examples of pairs, at short distances from each other, rising out of the parched pasture land. Others are shaped like watch-towers into the circular walls surrounding a prehistoric settlement. But are they actually look-out and defence posts? In the Bronze Age village of Ses Pahisses, near the little town of Artà in the east of Mallorca, the towers are to be found within the walls of the fortification, amongst the dwelling houses. Were they graves? Perhaps, for archaeologists have discovered human remains in many talayots. Or were they sun temples like the Sardinian nuraghi? The massive and clumsy central pillars at least make it quite clear that they were not dwellings. The huge stones in the middle would have been a great hindrance in everyday life. The talayots of Mallorca are still shrouded in mystery and no answer has yet been found to their riddle.

The taulas on Minorca, the small island to the east of Mallorca, only increase the complexity of the problem. Taulas (the word means 'tables') are the strangest T-shaped stone structures (see ill. 189), often of gigantic proportions. A slim, smoothly polished stone slab measuring six, eight or even ten metres rises vertically out of the ground; on top of it lies horizontally a similar but smaller slab. A ring of roughly hewn stone pillars encircle the taula. There is always a talayot nearby. What is the significance of these installations of which 18 have survived?* Because they seem to serve no practical purpose it might be assumed that they were religious sanctuaries or places of sacrifice. But if so, what was the religion and to whom did the builders make their sacrifices, and in any case, who were the builders?

* The most beautiful taulas are those at Talati, San Augustin, Vell, San Catlar, Torre d'en Gaumes and Trecupo.

189 The taula of Trepucó, not far from the little town of Mahón, is one of the 18 similar surviving T-shaped stone structures on Minorca.

There is also the problem of the Minorcan navetas, near the capital city Ciudadela, of which the most beautiful is D'es Tudons (see ill. 190). The roots of the name go back to the Spanish word 'nave' (ship), and it is true that with a little imagination the shape of an upturned boat can be recognized. Their purpose is known: they were graves. This is proved by the skeletons which were found in them. One naveta alone contained the remains of more than fifty people. But who built these peculiar charnel-houses and precisely why in the shape of an upturned boat? Are there any links with the Danish and southern Scandinavian Bronze Age burial ships, which were also designed to receive the dead? In their migration from northern Europe could the sea-farers have brought the idea to the Mediterranean? All this is nothing more than speculation.

190   The navetas which are found near the taulas are peculiar to Minorca. They are massive stone structures resembling an upturned ship. One of the most impressive is the naveta of d'es Tudons near the old capital of the island, Cuidadela.

Perhaps one day the archaeologists will be able to unravel the prehistoric mysteries of the Balearic Islands, but that presupposes years or even decades of hard work. And at this moment it is impossible to say with any certainty that this will produce any result.

In the summer of 1972 Friedrich Seick, an authority on
Morocco from Essen, implied that the experts in prehistory
and early history have treated not only the western
Mediterranean islands, but also the adjacent countries in a
very cavalier way. While it is true that his discovery does not
fit within the framework of a book on European prehistory,
nevertheless what he found is of such interest and might shed
such valuable light on the significance of the talayots and the
nuraghi on Sardinia, that it is worth while quoting the most
important part of his original publication: 'Near the middle of
the Atlantic coast of the kingdom of Morocco, some 80
kilometres south of Casablanca, between the resorts of
Azemour and El Jadida, there is a district which has a
completely unknown type of architecture, more like a relic of
architecture. Between the two above-mentioned places, south
of the river Oum or Rebia, Lighthouse No. 2 can be seen on
rising ground dominating the landscape.

'A good 300 metres away there are, quite surprisingly,
small circular structures (stalls), hidden in the bushes. And a
few minutes further on to the east, anyone on a ramble will
find large domed conical structures, which look like sugar-
loaves (see ill. 191 and 192). These are scattered haphazardly
over the landscape between the three villages of Sbeat, Amida
and Noasra. Many of them are empty, others are used as

*191 and 192 (opposite)
In 1972 in western
Morocco Friedrich Seick
discovered peculiar stone
structures which strongly
resemble the Sardinian
Nuraghi.*

stables and a very few still serve as dwellings. They stand
alone or in twos in the barren fields all but devoid of trees.

'The ground is infertile and covered only with stones and
rubble. Beneath this surface the cultivable soil is only a few
centimetres deep, but deep enough to be turned by a wooden
plough. This land also provides the building materials which
are in plentiful supply: the larger stones are piled up without
mortar to form circular rooms. The layers of stones do not
converge on a central point as is the case with a genuine dome
construction, but are gently tilted up (overhanging domes).

'In some of these buildings, either in the middle or on the
side, can be found small pits with a diameter of not more than
1.20 metres. The way down is through a bottle-necked
opening, and at the bottom it is possible to turn around in a
stooping position. The temperature in this region is said to be
so high during the heat following the harvest that the pit
protects any corn stored there from being eaten by insects.

'The inhabitants of this region and such property owners as
are still to be found – many of the buildings are abandoned –
call these stone dwellings tasotas. Apparently in prehistoric
times there were similar stone structures all round the
Mediterranean, from Palestine to the west coast of Portugal
and Spain. The resemblance of the tasotas to the already
mentioned nuraghi on Sardinia is striking. They have the

same external and internal forms, and above all they have the same parabola-shaped construction in the so-called artificial vault.

'In spite of certain nagging doubts, the thought cannot be summarily dismissed that in this region of Morocco, over a large area and over a long period an ancient form of dwelling has survived, about which nothing so far has been written.'

Were the nuraghi of Sardinia and the talayots of the Balearic Islands after all not temples, but mere dwellings?

The Prehistoric Temples on Malta

It would seem that each Mediterranean island had its own special and original prehistoric culture which can be seen in its own peculiar monuments. In Corsica there are the human-shaped menhirs, in Sardinia the nuraghi, Mallorca has its talayots, Minorca its taulas and navetas. Every year thousands of sight-seers are attracted to Crete and its rich remains of the Minoan civilization.

Malta and the neighbouring little island of Gozo are worthy links in this chain of Mediterranean islands with prehistoric remains. But that is the only connection between them. Because on Malta everything is different from Corsica, Sardinia or the Balearic Islands. The huge, almost majestic prehistoric structures of the little island were already 1,500 years old when the first nuraghi appeared on Sardinia and the first talayots on Mallorca. The Maltese monuments stretch back to the time when the menhirs on Corsica were still unhewn blocks of stone and possessed no human features.

That was 2800 B.C. and bronze and iron were still unknown on the island. Who the inhabitants of Malta and Gozo were at the time is unknown. But this unknown people constructed, without any metal tools, stone monuments which astonish us today. One of the largest of these structures is the temple of Hagar Qim (see ill. 193). It is situated two kilometres to the south-west of the village of Qrendi, in a most picturesque position on top of a group of hills high above the Mediterranean. From this magnificent vantage point it is possible to see as far as the steep cliffs of the neighbouring island of Filfla. The massive walls of the 4,500-year-old temple rise out of the reddish-brown earth and the green scented bushes like the walls of a labyrinth. There are gates which were worked out of a single boulder of rock more than two metres high; oval-shaped courtyards surrounded by walls more than twice the height of a man; passages and niches, single columns and large stone altars shaped like tables. On the south side, where the sea air with its salt content blows

unobstructed against the vertical slabs of soft globigerine chalk, the stone walls are weather-worn. Pocked with holes and strange hollows, they are at one and the same time a moving, impressive and timeless sight. It is such traces of time which make the visitor so conscious of the 4,500 years of the temple's existence. From Hagar Qim a narrow path, still high above the Mediterranean coast, and partly covered with slabs, leads gently downhill. It reaches Mnaidra after only a short kilometre. Here the landscape is even more isolated, even more grandiose, even more picturesque than at Hagar Qim. Far down below the breakers roll against the nearly vertical cliffs, an unending blue sky stretches over the island and far off the sea merges with the horizon. The earth is reddish brown, full of cracks covered with grey-green shrubs that smell heavily of a hundred different herbs. In the middle of this warm, brightly lit, barren area stand the stones of Mnaidra as if they had always stood there, as if they had been created together with the land in a time before time by a

193 The ruins of the four thousand five hundred year old temple of Hagar Qim on Malta.

temperamental god for whom the laws of time themselves had no meaning. It is unimaginable that within these walls, in front of these altars and stone chests, under the smooth vaults the remains of which can still be easily recognized, people once lived for whom all these niches and apses, the sacrificial tables with their irregular ornaments, had some significance. And yet it is true. But this period is 175 generations back and we do not know anything about the feelings of these people. We do not know with what desires or wishes they approached the temple of Mnaidra. Or was the whole building, like Hagar Qim, not a temple but a palace? Who can say with any certainty?

Hagar Qim and Mnaidra are not the only prehistoric monuments on Malta. In the north-west are to be found the two temples of Ta' Hagrat Mgarr, the oldest known megalithic structures on the island. Experts have dated them as being from between 2850 and 2800 B.C. In its ground plan the smaller building is amazingly like the old rock graves discovered by archaeologists in Xemxija on the north bank of Paul's Bay. Perhaps the builders did in fact want to imitate these graves and perhaps the small 'temple' of Ta' Hagrat Mgarr was also a last resting place fot the dead.

Only five kilometres from La Valetta, the capital of Malta, there is the Temple of Tarxien, quite close to the little village of the same name. Of the original four buildings, one is today almost completely destroyed. But the other three are truly splendid examples of the New Stone Age. The visitor is again confronted with a complicated combination of high walls, niches, recesses and chambers. Again there are single columns and altars, in this case richly ornamented. The main pattern of the mouldings is the spiral which played such a large role during the New Stone Age in Europe. But the prehistoric people of Tarxien also carved animals onto the blocks of stone: cattle, sheep, pigs and goats. Were these sacrificial animals brought to their gods? In a niche, separate from one of the altars, a long, sharp, flint blade was found. Was this a sacrificial knife?

Excavations have shown that the temple building of Tarxien had abruptly come to an end about 2,000 years B.C. A hostile people, armed with swords made of copper and spears with heads made of flint, overran the peaceable temple builders and usurped their place for five-and-a-half centuries. The invaders brought new religious rites with them. They cremated their dead and buried their ashes in urns in the temple of Tarxien.

A few miles north-west of Malta lies the island of Gozo.

This small island also has its prehistoric temple called Ggantija near the village of Xagtra. The two buildings of this temple embody – each in its own way – a prototype of Maltese prehistoric architecture. Two oval-shaped courtyards are situated next to each other. The entrance leads through the broad side into the first courtyard, a connecting passage leads on further into the second courtyard and in the opposite broad side of the second courtyard there is a semi-circular apse. In front of the entrance to the larger of the two temple buildings, there is a heavy stone slab in which there are six semi-circular shaped hollows. Close by stone balls were found which fitted exactly into these hollows. Some archaeologists believe that it is possible that the builders of the temples transported the massive slab on these simple ball-bearings, since the quarry from which the stone came is five kilometres further south near the coast.

The ancient inhabitants of the Maltese group of islands appear to have had a remarkable transport system. In many places on Malta and Gozo deep tracks like rails can be seen in the rocky ground. In places they are incised into the stone up to half a metre deep. They always run like two parallel tracks exactly the width of a wagon (see ill. 194). At certain points there are regular switch-boxes, branch lines and sidings. The two separate lines stretch far into the land and form a working network. Indeed experts on prehistory consider these strange double tracks in the rock to be a prehistoric traffic system. They believe that the vehicles which ran on these lines were a form of sledge. It is proved beyond doubt that this peculiar transport system dates from the New Stone Age or from the early period in which metal was used. In some places Phoenician graves ran diagonally across the stone grooves. Therefore the tracks in the rock must be older. Especially fine pairs of grooves with well-preserved sidings are to be found in the Minsija, which is an arid district to the north of the road from Birkirkara to St. Julian.

Perhaps the most beautiful and impressive monument on Malta is the Hypogeum of Pawla, a subterranean temple construction worked into the natural rock. This building is only comparable in the whole of the Mediterranean area with the domu de janas, the old rock graves of Sardinia (see ill. 176 and 288). Under the little town of Pawla the globerine chalk is certainly very soft, but what people were able to accomplish here between the years 2450 and 2400 B.C., without metal tools and only with stone wedges or with pointed horns or antlers, must fill the contemporary visitor with astonishment. The steps and rooms of the Hypogeum go three floors down

195 (opposite)   The
sacred shrine of the
Hypogeum of Malta looks
as if it had been made out
of gigantic hewn stones. In
fact it lies deep under
ground and was worked out
of the massive rock by the
ancient population almost
four-and-a-half thousand
years ago!

under the earth. Some prehistoric experts think that the hall
on the first level was the room of the oracles, because of the
unusual acoustics, which magnified any normally spoken
word to sound like a thundering roar, and also because of the
two small clay figures found here which were thought to
represent the faithful waiting for the words of the oracle. One
floor lower is the 'holy of holies' which some archaeologists
see as a place of religious rites and sacrifices (see ill. 195). From
there a narrow staircase leads down. Close to a wide pit the
corridor turns sharply to the left and through a door in the
rock the visitor reaches the lowest room of the sanctuary,
which is today thought to be the treasure chamber because its
approach was dangerous on account of the pit, which
constituted a serious hazard.

194   Mysterious double
tracks cover large areas of
Malta like a prehistoric
railway network.

Attempts by archaeologists to interpret the significance of the individual rooms of the Hypogeum of Pawla sound rather fantastic. The question arises, why did their colleagues all over the world accept these interpretations without too much grumbling, whereas many of them attacked such sound and scientifically based hypotheses as Spanuth's Atlantis theory, instead of treating them at least as possible working assumptions worthy of examination.

Whatever significance the subterranean rooms of the Hypogeum of Malta may have had, one thing remains certain: at some time in its history this structure must have been a burial place, because when it was excavated in the years following 1907 the experts found the remains of some 7,000 human beings.

Prehistory on the Fortunate Islands

'Storm turned into stone' – a Spanish poet once gave this description to the wild valley of Tejada in the heart of the Grand Canary Islands. As far as the eye can see, bizarre mountain columns stand out against the sky separated by 'barrancos', deep gorges with high, windswept walls. Here and there the knee-high and thick-stemmed shrubs of spurge withstand the storm which sweeps the summits of the highest mountains with trails of cloud. The rock needles of the Roques emerge out of massive cone-shaped stumps of greyish-brown lava, like unapproachable thrones of the gods. On one side is the massive cylinder-shape of the Bentaiga, on the other the oval columns of basaltic rock called the Fortaleza, and further on is a landmark of the island which dominates the whole scene, the gigantic Roque Nublo ('the rock in the clouds'), with the small stone 'Monk' at its side (see ill. 196). The landscape looks like a set for a mythological epic poem.

And, in truth, mythology does come alive here. The rock needles were in fact thrones of the gods! On the summits of the mountains there are traces of sacrificial sites and ritual shrines. A dilapidated path for climbers winds its way round the Roque Bentaiga which is 1,300 metres high. The way is hewn into the rock, but for hundreds of years no human foot trod on it. It leads to the summit of the heavy basalt rock, to an altar to which the ancient inhabitants once upon a time brought milk and honey as sacrifices. At the foot of the cylindrical rock there is a second altar and near it there are holy caves.

The other stone columns, which stand on the mountain summits like outsize natural menhirs, were also sanctuaries of

the ancient inhabitants of the Canary Islands. On the Roque Fortaleza and the Roque Palmés Narices and the Roque Nublo, which can be seen from afar, the ancient inhabitants of the island were as near to their god as on Bentaiga. Did these high towering stones not point directly to the shining incarnation of the gods in heaven?

196   In the centre of the island of Gran Canaria, the Roque Nublo, the seat of the gods, stands a pillar of basalt which the ancient inhabitants regarded as a sanctuary.

The ancient inhabitants of the Canary Islands worshipped the stars in the same way as some Bedouin tribes in Arabia do today, who believe that the sun created all life on earth and that the moon makes plants grow. On the rocks of the ancient sanctuaries and on the bulbous clay pots made by the inhabitants of the Canary Islands there were many scrawls representing the sun, the moon and stars (see ill. 196).

Who the inhabitants of the Canary Islands were, and where they came from is not known. Guide-books and popular scientific literature about the archipelago often called them Guanchen. But this is not correct, Guanchen were only one isolated tribe in the north of Tenerife. It is established that the original inhabitants were still living in the large and small Canary Islands when the Spanish conquerors overran them in the 15th century. It is also certain that the 'heathen barbarians', about whose culture the invaders did not bother for more than a century, had preserved and nurtured a rich legacy of the prehistoric Mediterranean tradition right up to about the time the Middle Ages were closing in Europe.

The ancient inhabitants of the Canary Islands did not belong to any single race. They must have settled on the islands at different periods. It can be assumed that the first of them landed on the archipelago with ships which had been driven onto the shores of the island by sea currents, and perhaps also by the wind. There was probably no way back. In ancient times sailors could hardly have battled against the main south-west current of the Canary Islands, which flows along the coast of north-west Africa. In this way, at various times during the prehistoric period and well into the classical age, separate groups coming from the Mediterranean area, must have landed on the shore of the 'Fortunate Islands', as they were known in ancient times. They travelled through the Straits of Gibraltar, or by the overland route to north-west Africa. They all made their individual cultural contribution. And because there was no return for them, and therefore they took no part in the further development of the ancient cultures of the Mediterranean area, the spiritual inheritance of the invaders of the Canary Islands remained almost unchanged for hundreds and thousands of years. Islands are too small to permit any great indigenous progress. They do not possess the many creative incentives which are available to a vastly more numerous continental population. The exchange of ideas with other countries is also lacking. The favourable climate also had its influence. The inhabitants of a country which Homer called the 'Elysian fields' do not need to be constantly changing and developing, they remain conservative in spirit.

All these circumstances make the Canary Islands a true museum of Mediterranean prehistory, a veritable mine in which traces of Stone Age culture can be found at every step. Many volumes could be written about the pre-Spanish history of the islands, and many unsolved riddles about the history of the ancient peoples in the Mediterranean area and in north Africa could be answered if the archaeological work on the Canary Islands were not still in its infancy.

It was due to Dominic Joseph Wölfel, the expert on the Canary Islands, who died in 1963, that the archaeological studies of the islands received a great impetus in this century. Spanish archaeologists, and especially the Institutum Canarium, which is an Austrian organization working on an international scale, are actively engaged in uncovering the immeasurable prehistoric treasures of the Canary Islands. Year by year they are finding new, fascinating sanctuaries, coming across so far undiscovered caves which were used as dwelling places, and excavating ceramics and statuettes on the island. But presumably only a few of the important sites have been discovered, and by no means all the finds have been evaluated. So far speculations about the cultural connections with the Mediterranean area of ancient times have produced few results.

The ancient inhabitants of the Canary Islands belong to a megalithic world. Their god, whom they named Alcorac or Alcoran, revealed himself in the stars. When Pope Clement VI sent missionaries to the islands he warned them of 'idolatrous heathen people of whom some worshipped the sun and others the moon'.

On the mountains sanctuaries were erected to the god of their star worship which they called Tagórors and Almogaren (see ill. 197 and 198). To these they brought mystical liquid

197   Above the ancient sacred meeting place of Cuatro Puerta, 5 kilometres west of the airport of Gando on Gran Canaria, on the top of a hill there is a place of sacrifice to which offerings of milk and honey were brought. It bears a close resemblance to the altar-stone shown in illustration 179.

198   The Tagóror of Cuatra Puertas, a place of worship and sacred meeting place of the ancient inhabitants of the Canary Islands.

199 and 200 (opposite)   The temple buildings of Cenobio de Valerón are situated in the north of the Island of Gran Canaria east of the little hamlets Galdar and Guìa.

offerings. These ceremonies were conducted by the Faycan, the arch-priest who was aided by vestalins or priestesses. In the north of the Gran Canaria, to the east of Guia, there is a mountain with a temple in which 365 cells have been carved out of the soft rock. It is called Cenobio de Valeron, and the vestalins lived in these cells (see ill. 199 and 200). On the top of the mountain above the whole construction, which resembles a honeycomb, there is a Tagóror.

Near the places of assembly for prayer in the open air the natives of the Canary Islands organized oracular caves, in which archaeologists discovered braziers and smoking pans. On particular days of the year the ancients visited the subterranean rooms to try to see the future in the smoke of the glowing fire. Superstition generally was very strong amongst the islanders. With burned clay they made small figures of animals, shaggy dogs, pigs, turkeys and hens which were supposed to be incarnations of the evil spirits. It is said that these unholy creatures appeared by night to the ancient inhabitants of the island.

The character of the religious rite, the worship of the stars, all point to aspects of the megalithic culture. But on the Canary islands there are no dolmen. Why should there be? Dolmen were artificially prepared graves. In the archipelago there was no lack of natural grottoes, and where there were none it was not difficult to make them out of the soft stone (see ill. 201 and 202). Dolmen would have been very unsuitable

201   On the road between the Cañadas and Vilaflor there is a cave dwelling used by the ancient inhabitants of Teneriffe.

constructions for the islands, for there are no big stone slabs which could be used as roofing slabs. But there are other stone arrangements which are common in megalithic times: small menhirs and little towers, shaped like the stumps of cones, measuring from 1.2 to 1.6 metres high, which were carefully erected from ochre-coloured narrow small slabs of stone. Both of these were inhabited by the souls of the forefathers and especially the tribal chieftains.

202   Prehistoric cave dwellings on Gran Canaria.

There is another clue which points definitely to the megalithic roots of the early civilization of the Canary Islands. On the menhirs and on the rocks of the sanctuaries there are constantly to be found scrawls of concentric circles and spirals, typical megalithic decorations. Particularly rich in this kind of symbolic ornament are the rock walls which surround the Grotto of Fuente de la Zarza, the 'well of the thorn-bush', a holy spring in the north-west of the little Canary Island of La Palma, not far from the village of Llano del Negro (see ill. 203 to 205). Do they not recall the carvings on the wall in the interior of the burial mound of Gavrinis in Brittany? (see ill. 147 on p. 194).

The link with the megalithic cultural heritage of the continent is not the only thing that the Fortunate Islands in the Atlantic have to offer the prehistorian. In the mountains on the islands there are inscriptions made up of simple

203   In north-west La Palma, in the middle of the isolated forest region of Fuente de la Zarza, is the 'Spring of the thorn bush'. Close to this sanctuary there is a grotto with prehistoric rock carvings. In the right foreground of this photograph two large spirals can be distinguished . . .

204   . . . Also on the walls near Fuente de la Zarza, spiral patterns are carved into the rock.

symbolic letters or signs representing syllables called 'Tarhas' (see ill. 39 on page 77). These remind the experts of ancient Mediterranean scripts of the seal and hieroglyphic writings and inscriptions of the early period in history in Crete, so that a connection cannot be excluded. Another type of script found in the Canary Islands indicates that there had been a connection between the islands and the mainland of northern Africa. The letters of the alphabet are very similar to those of the Berbers. A word, II O N + · (the sign should be written upwards, not as has been done here from left to right) was deciphered already as early as 1942. The sequence of letters can be reproduced with the word 'Irita', and in the language of the Berbers the word 'lereita' means '. . . has been here'.

At the beginning of the 1960s the Spanish expert on the Canary Islands, Sebastian Jimenez Sanchez, reported on finds of rock paintings on the islands. Until then the only megalithic symbols which had been known were those which had been scrawled on the rocks. Near Majada Alta and in the cave of Moro on Gran Canaria Sanchez discovered very stylized paintings of human figures which bear an amazing resemblance to the images on the Ahaggar mountains in southern Algeria, and to other paintings in north Africa and on the Spanish peninsula. The finds created the greatest stir

205   . . . The rock at the entrance of the cave is completely covered with ornamentation.

in professional circles, since they open the way to establishing further possible connections between the Mediterranean area and the Canary islands.

Were the Canary islands, which are a group of islands situated on the edge of Europe in the Atlantic Ocean facing the north-west coast of Africa, the furthest outposts of prehistoric European culture? Or was there a way beyond this boundary by which the ancient traditions were carried even further to the shores of the New World, as Thor Heyerdahl, who has been taken seriously by a number of experts, believes? The question is well worth debating, but it goes beyond the scope of this book, the limits of which have been set at the geographic outposts of Europe – the evidence of prehistory to be found in the stones of the Canary Islands.

MAPS

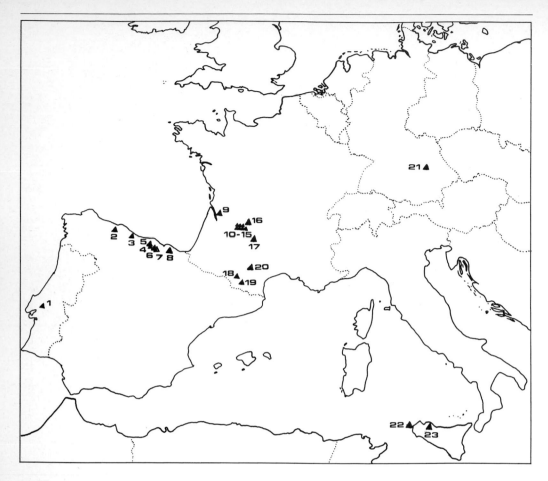

Map 1 – Important Ice Age Cave Paintings in Europe

1   *Escoural*
2   *Pena de Candamo* near San Remo de Candamo not far from Oviedo
3   *Pindal* near Unquera, not far from Llanes
4   *La Pileta* – near Benaojan not far from Ronda
5   *Altamira* near Santillana del Mar and Torrelavega
6   *El Castillo* near Puenta Viesgo, not far from Santander
7   *La Paseiga* near Puenta Viesgo, not far from Santander
8   *Santimamiñe* (also called *Basondo*) near Cortézubi and Guernica, not far from Bilbao
9   *Pair-non-Pair* near Marcamps and Bourg-sur-Gironde, not far from Bordeaux
10   *Bara-Bahau* (or *Barabao*) near Bugue and Les Eyzies-de-Tayac, not far from Périgueux
11   *Cap Blanc* near Laussel near les Eyzies-de-Tayac, not far from Périgueux
12   *Les Combarelles* near Les Eyzies-de-Tayac, not far from Périgueux

13   *Laugerie Basse* near Les Eyzies-de-Tayac, not far from Périgueux
14   *Rouffignac*, north of les Eyzies-de-Tayac, not far from Périgueux
15   *Cougnac* near Gourdon, not far from Sarlat
16   *Lascaux* near Montignac, not far from Brive
17   *Peche Merle* (also known as *Caberets*) near Caberets, not far from Cahors
18   *Le Mas-d'Azil* between Pamiers and St. Girons
19   *Niaux* near Tarascon-sur-Arriège
20   *Gargas* near Aventignon and Montrejeau not far from Tarbes
21   *Schulerloch* near Kelheim, not far from Regensberg (not very important, but only interesting in an overall survey of the best known Ice Age caves)
22   *Levanzo* on the island of the same name to the west of Sicily
23   *Addaura* on Monte Pellegrino near Palermo

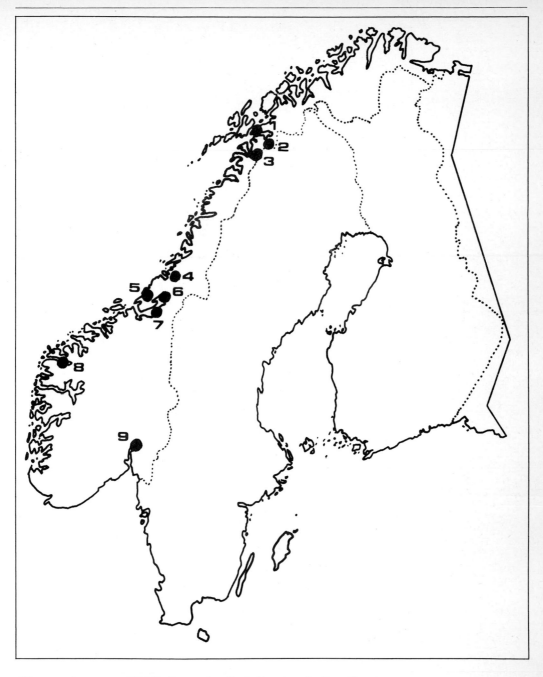

Map 2 – Important Middle Stone Age Rock Carvings in Scandinavia

1 *Sletjord* near Herjangen, Ofoten not far from Narvik
2 *Forselv* near Skjomen, Ofoten not far from Narvik
3 Leiknes near Tysfjord, not far from Narvik
4 *Böla* at Vallöy Farm near For not far from Stod, Nord-Tröndelag
5 *Hammer* near Beistad, 90 km north of Trondheim
6 *Bardal* near Beistad, north of Trondheim
7 *Evenhus* near Frosta on the Frosta peninsula at Trondheim-Fjord
8 *Vingen* near Rugsund, Davik, 90 km south of Alesund
9 *Ekeberg* not far from Oslo

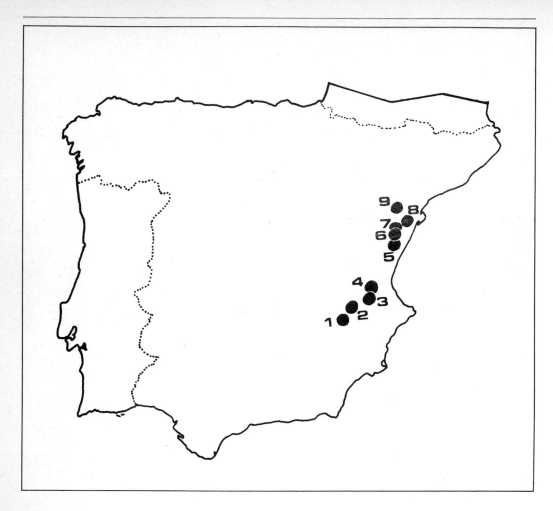

Map 3 – Important Middle Stone Age Rock Carvings in Eastern Spain

1 *Minateda* between Agramón and Hellin not far from Albacete
2 *Alpera* near Alpera between Albacete and Almansa
3 *Cueva de la Araña* near Bicorp, 80 km southwest of Valencia
4 *Dos Aguas* near Dos Aguas, 40 km southwest of Valencia
5 *Valtorta Cañon* between Albocácer and Tirig

6 *Gasulla Cañon* near Ares del Maestre not far from Albocácer
7 *Morella la Vella* near Morella not far from Albocácer
8 *Cueva de Polvorin* near Ulldecona not far from Tortosa
9 *Calapata* between Cretas and Calaceite not far from Tortosa

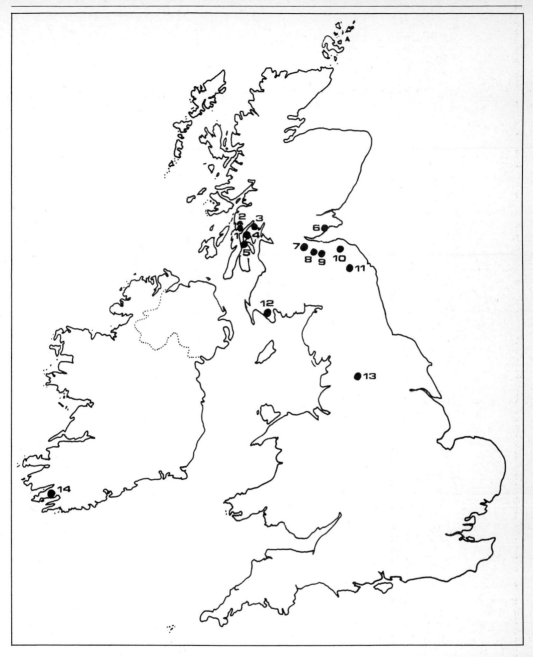

Map 4 – Important Find sites of Carved Stone Concentric Circles and other Designs Found in Britain

1 *Achnabreck* 3 km northwest of Lochgilphead, Argyll
2 *King's Cave* near Kilmartin northwest of Lochgilphead, Argyll
3 *Ardgowan* near Strachur on Loch Fyne, Argyll
4 *Ardmarnoch* near Kilfinnan on Loch Fyne, Argyll
5 *Point Farm* near Kilfinnan on Loch Fyne, Argyll
6 *Michael Colliery* near East Wemyss between Kircaldy and Leven on the Firth of Forth, Fife
7 *Castleton* near St Ninians, Stirling, 48 km west north west of Edinburgh
8 *Bonnington Mains* near Ratho, Midlothian, 13 km west of Edinburgh

9 *Hawthornden* near Lasswade, Midlothian, 10 km south west of Edinburgh
10 *Taprain Law* near Prestonkirk (East Lothian) not far from Haddington
11 *Roughting Linn*, Northumberland, 14 km west of Belford
12 *Drumtroddan* between Port William and Wigtown
13 *Panorama Stone and Swastika stone* on Ilkley Moor not far from Bradford, West Riding
14 *Derrynablaha* near Kenmare, County Kerry

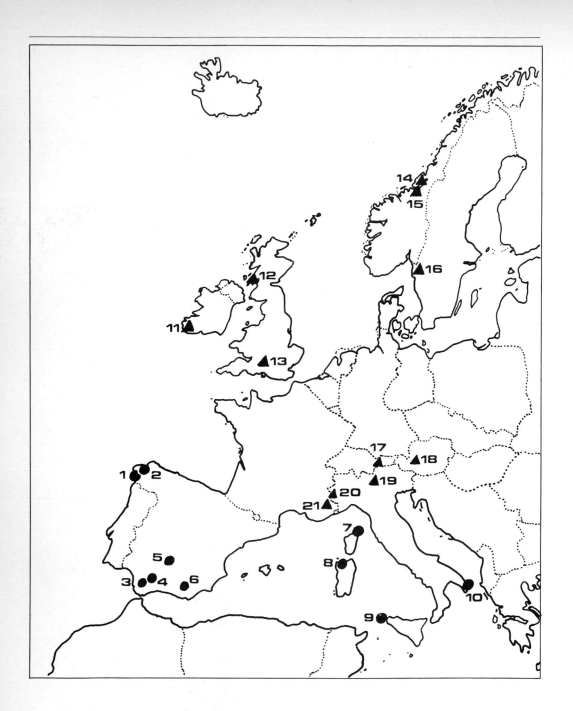

Map 5 – Important European Late Stone Age Rock Carvings (●) and those of The Bronze and Ice Ages (▲)

1 *Pedra das Ferraduras*, Fentans, 20 km northwest of Pontevedra
2 *Palvorin* near Coruña
3 *Tajo de las Figuras* near the ruined cloisters of El Cuervo on the shores of the Laguna de la Janda in the Casas Viejas area
4 *La Pileta*, 12 km west of Ronda not far from Algeciras
5 *Fuencaliente* near Fuencaliente 50 km north of Montoro
6 *Cuevas de los Leteros* near Vélez Blanco, 90 km north of Almeria
7 *Grotto Scritta* near Olmeta in the Bastia area
8 *Tomba Branca* near Sassari
9 *Levanzo*, on the island of the same name west of Sicily
10 *Romanelli* near Castro, Apulia
11 *Derrynablaha* near Kenmare, County Kerry

12 *Achnabreck* 3 km northwest of Lochgilphead, Argyll
13 *The White Horse of Uffington*, Berkshire, 29 km south-west of Oxford
14 *Bardal* near Beitstad, 80 km northwest of Trondheim
15 *Lierfall* near Stjördal, east of Trondheim
16 *Extensive important find sites* around Tanum in Bezirk, Bohuslan
17 *Carschenna*, Hochalm, east of Sils, Graubenden Canton
18 *Holl* in Toten Gebirge near Liezen, 100 km south of Linz
19 *Valcamonica* north of Lago Iseo, an area of many important find sites, especially at Naquane near Capo di Ponte
20 *Val Chissone* west of Pinerolo
21 *Mont Bego* near St Delmas de Tende 50 km northwest of Nice

BIBLIOGRAPHY

Anati, Emmanuel: *Camuna Forschung 1*; Capo di Ponte (Brescia), 1974. Centro Camuno di Studi Preistorici

Anati, Emmanuel: *Evoluzione e Stile nell' Arte Rupestre Camuna*; Capo di Ponto (Brescia), 1975. Centro Camuno di Studi Preistorici

Biedermann, H. und Schwarz-Winkelhofer, J.: *Das Buch der Zeichen und Symbole*, Graz; 1972. Verlag für Sammler

Bord, Janet and Colin: *Mysterious Britain*; London, 1973. Garnstone Press Ltd.

Brogna, Cesare Giulio: *Arte Rupestre Preistorica e Metodi di Rilevamento*; Pinerolo. Cesare Borgna

Borgna, Cesare Giulio: *La Mappa Litica di Rocio Clapier*; in "L'Universo" Jahrgang XLIX, 1969. Instituto Geografico Militaire, Firenze

Borgna, Cesare Giulio: *Studio metodico-cronologico del repertorio di sculture preistoriche della zóna de Fentans-Galizia Spagna*; in "Cuadernos de Estudios Gallegos", Tomo XXVIII, 1973. Tallers Graficos Vda. De C. Bermejo, Madrid

Burgstaller, E.: *Felsbilder und Inschriften im Toten Gebirge in Oberösterreich.*

Gadow, Gerhard: *Der Atlantis-Streit*; Frankfurt 1973. Fischer Taschenbuch Verlag

Glob, P. V.: *Vorzeit Denkmäler Dänemarks*; Nuemünster, 1967, Karl Wachholtz Verlag

Glory, A.: *Caverne ornée de Bara-Bahau*; Le Bugue, 1955. Bara-Bahau

Grosjean, Roger: *La Corse avant l'Histoire*; Paris, 1966, Editions Klinksieck

Grosjean, Roger: *Filitosa, haut lieu de la Corse préhistorique*, Corse, 1973. Centre de Préhistoire Corse

Hadingham, Evan: *Ancient Carvings in Britain: A Mystery*; London. Garnstone Press Ltd.

Harbison, Peter: *Guide to the National Monuments in the Republic of Ireland*; Gubb and Macmillan, Dublin, 1975

Institutum Canarium: *Almogaren, Band I bis IV*; Hallein, Austria, 1970 ff. Institutum Canarium

Institutum Canarium: *I.C.-Nachrichten Nr. 9 bis 20*; Hallein, Austria, 1972 ff. Institutum Canarium

Isetti, M. Louis G.: *Les gravures préhistoriques du Mont-Bego*; Cuneo 1974. Institut International d'Etudes Ligures

Keisch, Bernhard: *Secrets of the Past: Nuclear Energy Applications in Art and Archaeology*; U.S. Atomic Energy Commission, 1972

Keisch, Bernhard: *Lost Worlds: Nuclear Science and Archaeology*; U.S. Atomic Energy Commission, 1973

Kühn, Herbert: *Die Felsbilder Europas*; Stuttgart 1971, Verlag W. Kohlhammer

Kühn, Herbert: *Vorgeschichte der Menschheit, Band 1 bis 3*; Köln, 1962, 1963, 1966. Verlag M. DuMont Schauberg, Köln

Larsen, Bodil Leth: *Möns Vorzeitdenkmäler*; Mön, Dänemark. Møns Turist forening

Lilliu, Giovanni: *La Civilitá dei Sardi dal Neolitico all' Età dei Nuraghi*, Turino, 1967. Edizione Rai Radiotelevisione Italiana

Lukan, Karl: *Alpenwanderungen in der Vorzeit*; Wien 1965. Verlag Anton Schroll & Co.

Maxia, Carlo: *La Civiltà Megalitica nuragica rilevata con l'astroarcheologia*; Firenze, 1973. Instituto Geografico Militare

Minvielle, Pierre: *Guide de le France Souterraine*; Paris, 1970. Tchou Editeur

Morris, Ronald W. B.: *The Cup-and-Ring Marks and similar Sculptures of Scotland*; in "Proceedings of the Society of Antiquaries of Scotland", Vol. 100, 1967–1968. Society of Antiquaries of Scotland

Morris, Ronald W. B.: *The Petroglyphs at Achnabreck, Argyll*; in "Proceedings of the Society of Antiquaries of Scotland", Vol. 103, 1970–1971. Society of Antiquaries of Scotland

Müller, Rolf: *Der Himmel über dem Menschen der Steinzeit*; Berlin, 1970. Springer Verlag

Paschetta, Vincent: *Merveilles-Tende-Gordolasque*; Grenoble, 1974. Librairie Didier et Richard

Sarradet, Max: *Font-de-Gaume en Périgord*; Périgueux, 1971. Pierre Fanlac Editeur

Savona, Comune di: *Mostra internazionale d'arte rupestre*; Savona, 1974. Comune di Savona

Stacul, Giorgio: *Arte della Sardegna Nuragica*; Milano, 1971. Arnoldo Mondadori Editore

Süss, Emmanuele: *Rock Carvings in the Valcamonica*; Milano, 1954. Edizione del Milione

Taralon, Jean: *Lascaux; Paris, 1961.* Caisse Nationale des Monuments Historiques

Thom, Alexander: *Megalithic Sites in Britain*; London. Oxford University Press, 1967

Wolf, Karl Felix: *Dolomitensagen, 13 Auflage*; Innsbruck, 1974. Tyrolia verlag

Zindel, Christian: *Zu den Felsbildern von Carschenna*; in "Jahresbericht 1967 der Historische-Antiquarischen Gesellschaft von Graubünden". Historisch-Antiquarische Gesellshcaft, Chur

PICTURE CREDITS

INDEX